D0856408

Party Food

A Partisan History of Food & Farming in America

R.C. Harris

Party Food

A Partisan History of Food & Farming in America

R.C. Harris

COMMON GROUND

First published in 2021
as part of the *Food Studies* Book Imprint
doi:10.18848/978-1-86335-248-2/CGP (Full Book)

Common Ground Research Networks
University of Illinois Research Park
Champaign, IL
61820

Copyright © R.C. Harris 2021

All rights reserved. Apart from fair dealing for the purposes of study, research, criticism or review as permitted under the applicable copyright legislation, no part of this book may be reproduced by any process without written permission from the publisher.

Library of Congress Cataloging-in-Publication Data

Names: Harris, R.C., 1972- author.
Title: Party food : a partisan history of food & farming policy in America
  / R.C. Harris.
Description: Champaign, IL : Common Ground, [2021] | Includes
  bibliographical references and index. | Summary: "Food writers commonly
  exhort their readers to "vote with their fork" in support of a
  progressive food policy agenda. However real voting involves supporting
  political parties, and most people do not know the political history of
  food. This book examines Democratic and Republican approaches to food
  policy in the spirit of helping the foodies and farmers see where things
  stand. The book introduces the reader to the political game of food
  policy in order to explain "Red" and "Blue" history with food policy.
  This work introduces the political context for understanding partisan
  food policy history: the "business" of farming and the "sport" of team
  politics in American government. It tells the story of Democratic and
  Republican support for farm and food policies, with the observation that
  farm and food policy is essentially a social welfare policy-a
  traditional party fault line. The book uses original research to present
  the activities of Democrat and Republican Congressional Representatives,
  Presidents/USDA administrators and Party Platforms"-- Provided by
  publisher.
Identifiers: LCCN 2021025381 (print) | LCCN 2021025382 (ebook) | ISBN
  9780949313829 (hardback) | ISBN 9781863352475 (paperback) | ISBN
  9781863352482 (pdf)
Subjects: LCSH: Food habits--Political aspects--United States. | Nutrition
  policy--United States. | Agriculture--Political aspects--United States.
  | Political parties--United States.
Classification: LCC GT2853.U6 H37 2021 (print) | LCC GT2853.U6 (ebook) |
  DDC 394.1/20973--dc23
LC record available at https://lccn.loc.gov/2021025381
LC ebook record available at https://lccn.loc.gov/2021025382

Cover Photo Credit: R.C. Harris

Table of Contents

Dedication

To farmers, foodies and the public servants who work for us

Acknowledgments

I would like to briefly thank those who taught me political science at the University of Illinois-Urbana Champaign so many years ago. I still hear their guidance in the puzzles I research today. I would also like to acknowledge those recent peers who have taken the time to critically engage my work, most notably my anonymous reviewers and Christopher Bosso. Their generous expert attention has strengthened my scholarship and my communication of my science. I would also like to thank my editors, Kerry Dixon and Ebony Jackson, for all of the professional assistance at every step and Common Ground Research Networks Food Studies Book Imprint for giving me this platform. Finally, I would like to acknowledge my students in my food policy courses in the Williams School at Washington and Lee University. Their dedicated study and engaging discussion has provided significance for the work I do and for the subject I profess.

Preface

Vote with your fork. It is a common mantra among food writers. They exhort their readers to support a particular food policy agenda by eating a certain way: eat local to support the farmer down the road, eat plants to save the planet, and so on. However, real voting involves politics, and little has been written about the comprehensive political picture of food policy—the one citizens engage in— namely *voting for elected officials.* Moreover, politics is not free form. It is mediated by political parties that translate political votes into political action. Furthermore, most citizens tend to participate in voting with a team mentality, consistently favoring one political party more than the other in their political judgments. When it comes to American political parties, Democrat and Republican, where should a foodie turn? Or what about a real minority, like a conventional commercial farmer? Which party is the farmers' party? Surprisingly, the answer is not as clear as one might think. While something in our gut may tell us that foodies will be more at home in the blue party (Democrats) and that farmers will be more at home in the red party (Republicans), is it really because of partisan approaches to food policy? Might it not be because values other than food policy lead foodies to lean Democrat and farmers to lean Republican?

Ask yourself this: *What is the Democratic and Republican position on food and farming policy?* That is the central question of this book. Interestingly enough, the experts who study party politics, political scientists like myself, tell us they don't have one. They refer to food and farming policy as one of the rare examples of *bipartisanship* in American politics. In other words, the experts say that political parties do not meaningfully distinguish themselves on food and farming policy. Really? It seems to me an important issue is being left on the table, *IF* this is the case. Citizens care deeply about food. Empires have been toppled in food riots. Emperors of old understood that having enough bread was the first priority for retaining power. Political parties should not be too complacent when it comes to food policy.

I disagree with the experts. I believe food policy is much more partisan than they are telling us, and I am writing this book to let the foodies and farmers know where things stand. So what is the partisan history of food? What is the relationship between the Democratic Party and farm policy? How about Republicans, are they really the enemy of foodies? Are the experts right—is there little to distinguish them? *Just how partisan is food policy?* How do we find out?

As a social scientist, I judge reality based on action. That means the place to start is with the activities of the actual partisans in power—Representatives, Senators, Presidents—as well as the stated positions of the parties themselves—the Democratic and Republican party platforms. Have Democrats and Republicans behaved differently when it comes to food policy?

Believe it or not, all of the influential foodie books in recent years neglect any meaningful exploration of partisan behavior in food policy. *The Omnivore's Dilemma* (Michael Pollan 2006), *Food Inc.* (Peter Pringle, 2003), *Fast Food Nation* (Eric Schlosser, 2001)—none of these discuss party behavior and food policy, and the words "Democrat" and "Republican" do even register in the index of the first two. Even the scholars neglect political parties. Nutritionist Marion Nestle's *Food Politics: How the food industry influences nutrition and health* (University of California, 2013*)*, a giant in the field, does not discuss partisan approaches to food policy. Economist Jason Lusk's conservative critique of Nestle and Pollan, *Food Police: A well-fed manifesto about your plate* (Crown Forum, 2013*)*—ditto. Even the policy experts missed this. Political scientist Robert Paarlberg's *Food Politics: What Everyone Needs to Know* (Oxford, 2013)—nothing. Renowned agricultural economist, James L. Novak and colleagues' *Agricultural Policy in the United States* (Routledge 2015)—zip. The last good discussions of political parties and food policy are found as secondary stories in political science books about something else, namely interest group and lobbyist behavior in food and farming policy (e.g. Sheingate 2001; Hansen 1993).

Part of the problem is that political science taught generations of experts that political parties do not matter. However, to the average voter and citizen, that just does not ring true. Parties must matter or voters would not be attached to (or repulsed by!) them. Parties must matter or leaders in government would not try to organize partisan agendas to impress or satisfy said voters. The experts used to think we needed *more* partisan behavior, calling it *responsible party government.* Now the experts lament strong parties, referring to them derogatory terms, like *polarized.* Polarized parties imply voters have a clear choice, that their positions are *poles* apart. Is this true in food policy? Do Democrats and Republicans vote differently, pursue different goals? If so, what are they? What *is* the partisan agenda when it comes to food and farming policy? And, if they are polarized, how can the experts continue to refer to food policy as bipartisan?

There is more at stake here than just voting with your fork. If food policy is partisan and poles apart, instability is more likely. To the extent government control swings pendulum-like from one extreme agenda to another, food policy could descend into chaos—and that's not good. Emperors needed bread. Nations need food. To know if we are in trouble or on the right track to effective policy management, we must look closer at the political story of food, and, in my opinion, we must understand where the real fault lines are.

This book is designed to explore the political history of food and agriculture policy to understand historic partisan approaches to food politics. Scholars of *politics* tend to focus on pluralism, the belief that interest group behavior and lobbying drives everything, feeling that political parties were dead and not helpful. Scholars of *policy* tend to focus on presidents, or more accurately, presidential administrations, when they discuss food policy. Both approaches fail to acknowledge that political parties, not interest groups, recruit candidates and organize elections, that political parties coordinate government efforts within Congress and across chambers and branches, and that political parties are *the number one* identifying factor in voter choice. So what about political parties and partisan approaches over time? *Is there a red or blue approach to food and farm policy? If so, why?* The question requires an investigation of Democrat and Republican behavior toward food policy, and the answers may surprise you.

Some thoughts on Preparing to read this Book

What a history of partisan food policy means. Party Food is a history of political parties and food. The majority of the book will catch you up on the game—the historic team rivalries in this particular policy area—so you can understand the backstory of the politics of today. The issues motivating the rivalries are surprisingly technical for farm policy. Such things as banks, currency, loan rates and "parity" may not sound sexy, but they are the stuff of bitter partisan contests, violent mobs, and instant switches in the political fortunes of presidential candidates.

Why teams matter. A portion of the book adds to the conversation on food politics by adding the notion of competitive political teams. If policy is understood as the outcome of competitive *team play*, it makes more sense. Contemporary food books argue that it is the outcome of competitive *interests*, such as environmentalists, foodies, farmers, and the food industry. However, in the context of this book, such interests are just the sponsors of the game and the fans in the stands. The real action, making plays and scoring goals, is accomplished on a field of *competitive team play*. So what happens there? What does that look like? Well, to understand the game, you have to understand the players, their positions, the rules (constraints on play for a particular player), the way a particular team is fielded (elections and politics), the seasonal calendar (election cycles), and the role of leadership both on and off the field. It is even more interesting when you consider that one team always has fewer players than the other team, and that "fantasy" farm bloc teams— teams formed from drafting small numbers from *both* sides—is the norm! You can follow the game of lobby groups (or "sponsors" as I call them), but if you don't understand the partisan game, the actual victories (or losses) might not make much sense.

Heroes of Farm Policy—the battle for our progressive and conservative values. Some of the book also names the "Heroes and Villains" of legacy New Deal farm support policy. Presidents (Including Trump, Obama and 2020 hopefuls) are given a voice to provide us with the unique flavor of farm & food rhetoric—and their words provide interesting analysis for the picture of food policy today. Political scientists feel the New Deal/Great Society and Civil Rights explain today's major party divisions. Farm and food policy is no different, and the issues of government intervention (for the economy, for poverty, and for human rights) provide a bedrock disagreement between the two teams, especially if human rights and economic interventions include the environment. These government interventions solidified a turn from classical liberal notions of private property, individualism, liberty and *limited* (not constantly *intervening!*) government in food production. These classical values become associated with the party seeking to *conserve* them—the contemporary Republican Party. The more *progressive* sentiments of harnessing government for the greater good also overturned the notion of farmers and ranchers making independent production decisions with private sector (and some public sector!) resources, perhaps reducing them to mere laborers for agribusiness and redefining their property (capital and means to production) as a public environmental resource. Farmers might resent this progressive picture of what they do and who they are—even if they want a level playing field with corporations and even if they desire to be proper stewards of natural resources. They might view *food production as a public resource* they willingly provide.

The power of the consumer voter to shape food values. The private sector (then and now) grew, produced, packaged, wholesaled and retailed food in a generally competitive market. Food values would necessarily reflect the values of those doing the work—both farmers and those in the broader industry. If those doing the work were motivated by profit, food values become *what is profitable* for those with the labor & capital to produce food. And what is profitable? *Food that sells.* In this backdoor way, food consumers control food values by what they purchase, as their preferences make for profit. Food which is *priced right* also sells, and government policy can make some foods more expensive than others. What else is profitable? Food which is *sustainable* over the long haul and *efficient*, too—and in the sense of the market—*priced* sustainably. In the struggle for free market versus government control, the food industry tries to manipulate consumers & government through all the commercial and political channels possible. However, consumers not only control industry with their preferences, consumers control government as voters. And, government can push back on industry with team play by protecting members from sponsor pressure to pursue team political goals. In this way, the conclusion that industry dominates is not foregone. Most recently, *moral food sells* and again, industry and government have responded to the consumer citizen to support this—picking up on notions of social justice, food democracy, fair trade worker protection, etc.

Introduction

Farming and food production has always been political. Farmers want to be part of who gets what, when from government. Consumers want to meet their needs, ideally on their own terms. Political parties are the normal way such values get translated into policy demands, but most experts consider farm politics bipartisan—meaning that divisions and disagreements in farm policy are not normally along *partisan* lines, with Democrats on one side and Republicans on the other. In the experts' view, political divisions in farm policy have typically been more along the lines of geography, as producers of different crops competed for government goodies. Different food items tend to be grown in different parts of the nation, so government representatives naturally supported local producers— wheat in the Plains, corn in the Midwest, dairy in Wisconsin and Pennsylvania, cotton in the South, fruits and vegetables in California, and so on. Thus, Congressional representatives from different parts of the country would work together, regardless of party to protect local producers.

Our Food Values

However, there *is* more at stake than geography and local economies. Politics is the allocation of values and resources, and food and farm policy is no different. So what exactly *are* our values at this moment? Obviously we value those farm products mentioned above. However, farm production has political ties to other mainstream political concerns—and these have much more partisan implications. Food is typically produced in the rural countryside, so farm policy effects rural economic development. Farming is also the foundation of the nation's food supply, so farm policy influences the general welfare, especially *if* we eat, *what* we eat and *how much* it costs. Moreover, farming is dependent on the environment for production and its location in the countryside means that farming has a large environmental footprint. These mainstream political concerns are fellow political travelers with farm policy, and modern food and farm policy has pursued farm economic and production goals alongside rural development, human nutrition and conservation goals.

The Logic of the Farm Bill

Most formally, these values can be seen in the "omnibus" (or "catch-all") nature of the Farm Bill, passed every five years or so to pursue these goals. While most citizens may think only lawyers can decipher legislation, the logic of the farm bill is actually quite simple. *It is just a neat and tidy list of our food production values.* We value wheat, corn, soybeans, cotton, peanuts, sugar, etc. These are promoted under the *Commodities* title. We value protecting our soil, water, and wildlife. These are promoted under the *Conservation* title. We value exporting our bounty to other nations for a profit, and we value providing food aid to nations in need. These are promoted under the *Trade* title. We value making sure our own citizens are healthy and get enough to eat, perhaps using the Supplemental Nutrition Assistance Programs (formerly known as "food stamps"). These are promoted under the *Nutrition* title. We value providing access to credit so farmers can purchase supplies and land. This is promoted under the *Credit* Title. We value strong rural communities, since that is where most food production occurs, and we want them to have the infrastructure to prosper. This is promoted in the *Rural Development* title. We value nutrition and agricultural research to keep us healthy and to keep food production innovative. This is promoted in the *Research* title. We value the sustainable development of timber resources. This is promoted in the *Forestry* title. We value energy conservation in agricultural production and the development of bio-energy sources. This is addressed in the *Energy* title. We value fruits and vegetables and flowers and landscaping. These are promoted in the *Horticulture* Title. We value risk management for food production which largely depends on unpredictable variables, such as weather, pest and disease outbreaks. This is promoted in the *Crop Insurance* title. There is even a title for everything we've missed, such as livestock and poultry and honey bees and wool production, not to mention supporting young, women or minority food producers. These various and sundry values are promoted in the aptly named *Misc.* Title. All in all, the *2014 Farm Bill* had twelve titles (or sub-sections) speaking to major and minor goals in farm policy. *See Table 1.*

Table 1. 2014 Farm Bill and Budget Allocations (Percentage of total budget)

Title I.	Commodities	$44.4 Billion (4%)
Title II.	Conservation	$57.6 Billion (6%)
Title III.	Trade	$3.5 Billion
Title IV.	Nutrition (SNAP/Food stamps)	$756.4 Billion (79%)
Title V.	Credit	(-$2.0 Billion)
Title VI.	Rural Development	$.2 Billion
Title VII.	Research	$1.2 Billion
Title VIII.	Forestry	$.0 Billion
Title IX.	Energy	$1.1 Billion
Title X.	Horticulture (Fruit and Vegetables)	$1.7 Billion
Title XI.	Crop Insurance	$89.8 Billion(9%)
Title XII.	Misc. (Livestock, poultry, etc.)	$2.3 Billion
	Total	$956.4 Billion(98%)

Source: Congressional Research Service *The 2014 Farm Bill (P.L. 113-79)*
Summary and Side-by-side
Notes: The Credit title actually makes money, generating $2 billion *in revenue* under this bill. The Forestry title only allocated $13 *million.*

Teasers from 2014

Politics is the allocation of values and resources, and food policy is no different. The values of the nation are translated into federal spending and program budgets as the key method to implementing farm policy. To see the amount of resources the federal government allocates to these values, *Table I* presents the budget allocations. Looking at these numbers, it is obvious that four values dominate our food policy: Nutrition assistance, Crop insurance subsidies, Conservation programs, and Commodities subsidies. These four titles make up *ninety-eight percent* of the federal food bill budget. Thus, in terms of who gets what, the farm bill is really about social welfare food programs (about 80%) and farmer subsidies for commodities and insurance (about 13%).

Party Food?

So what about politics? Just how partisan is this stuff? Do Democrats and Republicans share the same food values, or do they value different things? Interestingly enough, unlike 2018, politics gave us a natural experiment to clearly see Democrat and Republican priorities at play in the 2014 Farm Bill. As we will discuss later, political parties are teams that compete for votes to win office and score policy goals. That year was a midterm election year, with all of the House and one-third of the Senate up for re-election. The teams wanted to keep their players on the field and win elections. Each party controlled part of Congress: the Republicans controlled the House, the Democrats controlled the Senate. This farm bill was passed in an election year, so each party was competing for votes by showcasing their policy values to the nation.

As you will learn later in the book, understanding *food* politics requires you to understand *politics* first, so I must give you a little insider information. In general, House bills tend to be *more* partisan and extreme than Senate bills because Senate rules and traditions require *more* compromise to get things done. Compromise bills between the chambers are hammered out by the two chambers in conference committees, so that a unified *Conference Bill* can be voted on and presented to the president. As a rule, the final versions of compromise bills tend to more closely reflect the values of the Senate.

Different Party, Different Meal

Comparing the 2014 House version of the farm bill (Republican) to the Senate version of the farm bill (Democrat) gives us a rough idea of the partisan disagreements between Democrats and Republicans. I might get a little technical here, but the rest of the book explains the politics as a story. This is just the "teaser" to test for partisanship with a little math. Since politics is the allocation values and resources, the simplest comparison is the difference in Republican and Democratic allocation of federal dollars in food policy. *Table 2* provides a side-by-side comparison of proposed new spending levels for the major titles.

Doing the Math

As might be expected, Democrats and Republicans were split on the major issues. Both sides agreed that government spending needed to be reduced and retargeted. However, they varied significantly in *where* to cut and by *how* much. The most dramatic difference is social welfare spending for nutrition—notably SNAP. Here, Democrats sought a slight reduction (half a percent or $4 billion dollars), while Republicans wanted *ten times* as much (five percent or $40 Billion dollars). Less dramatically, Democrats tried to keep more conservation dollars than Republicans. In terms of direct farmer assistance, both parties wanted to increase crop insurance programs, but Republicans would have increased spending at almost *twice* the amount of Democrats. Both parties also wanted to wean farmers from direct commodity payments, with Democrats slightly less so. Interestingly enough the conference version increased commodity spending above chamber levels! (Perhaps my colleagues who study lobbyists are on to something).

Table 2. Comparison of Republican and Democratic 2014 Farm Bill Spending
(As a departure from previous levels)

Budget Outlay	Republican (House version)	Democrat (Senate Version)	Final Bill (Conference Version)
Crop Insurance $	10% more	6% more	6.7% more
Nutrition $	5% less	.05% less	1% less
Commodities $	32% less	29% less	24% less
Conservation $	8% less	5% less	6% less

Source: Gross numbers provided by Congressional Research Service
The 2014 Farm Bill (P.L. 113-79) Summary and Side-by-side. Percentages here
are the author's calculations.

The second part of the experiment is to look at how Representatives and Senators actually voted on the bills. To keep score—so to speak—to see if these are polarizing or meaningful differences between Democrats and Republicans. More insider stuff: political scientists define polarizing votes as those votes where the majority of one party votes *against* the majority of the other party. By contrast, if these votes were bi-partisan, they should gain votes from members of both parties. Notice these were chamber bills. So what about individual Democrats and Republicans in each chamber? Did any Democrats support the House (Republican) bill? Did any Republicans support the Senate (Democratic) bill? If so, how many? This will help us sort out if the farm bill was bipartisan or polarized.

It wouldn't make sense to tease us with the 2014 Farm Bill if there was no story, so sure enough, the parties behaved differently on their farm bill votes. On the House side no Democrats—not one—voted for the House Bill. In contrast, almost all of the Republicans (95%) supported the House Bill. How's *that* for polarization? Furthermore, the House remained divided on the compromise bill. When the watered-down Conference version came up for a vote, the one that would go to the *Democratic* President, only a minority of House Democrats (43%) supported it, even though it looked a lot like what the Senate Democrats wanted. That same compromise bill lost some support among Republicans for the same reason it gained Democrat support. Over a quarter of the House Republicans (27%) voted against it. Since both teams voted in opposite directions, the experts would have to concede the parties clearly differed on this bill.

Senators Don't Always Have Math

In the Senate, things are slightly different. The Senate version of the bill was the result of a *unanimous consent agreement* among the Senators—a common tool for many Senate bills. Senators may not agree with the bill but they consent not to block its passage and no vote is recorded. The bill is simply passed by "Unanimous Consent". No individual Senator has to go on record as for or against the bill. However, when it came time to vote on the conference bill, which closely approximated the original Democratic Senate spending levels, less than half (48%) of Senate Republicans supported it. By contrast, most (83%) of Senate Democrats supported the conference bill. Again, no bipartisanship here.

Different Parties, Different Food Agendas

Other food and farming bills of recent times show a similar lack of bipartisanship. The 2010 Healthy Hunger-Free Kids Act (commonly associated with First Lady Michelle Obama's anti-obesity initiative) funded school lunches and other programming, but found support mostly among fellow Democrats. Similarly, the 2016 GMO federal food labeling law, which preempted more stringent state-level GMO labeling laws, was supported by mainly by Republicans. It appears that just these brief current events point to polarization in food policy, with Democrats and Republicans clearly offering different food agendas to the American public.

So Where Do We Begin?

A few preliminaries are in order for us to get a useful picture of food and agriculture politics and partisan behavior. We need to understand a little about farming and where the farmers are coming from—for their demands are what started the Farm Bill process in the first place. We need to understand a little about political parties and where Democrats and Republicans are coming from— for their policy orientations shape their approach to food politics. We also need to understand the way experts approach political parties and why they can't decide if they want strong (polarized) parties or not.

Once we lay this groundwork, we can begin to examine the story of Democratic and Republican food agendas. We will look at Congress. We will look at presidents. We will look at party platforms. All the while, we will compare the Democratic and Republican approach to food and farming policy.

While I am at it, I might as well give you the punch lines—so you know exactly where we are headed. This book makes several observations largely ignored by food writers and policy experts in their discussion of American agriculture. First, farm policy is social welfare policy. Fellow political scientist, Adam Sheingate first made this argument with regard to farmers, and I plan to pursue it vigorously and more broadly in this discussion. Second, because Democrats and Republicans have very distinct positions on social welfare policy, there is no *real* bipartisanship in food policy. I am indebted to Robert Smith and Richard Seltzer for their nudge in this direction, though their book does not discuss food policy. Third, the political parties have quite clear statements on food policy, and their agendas are no secret, if one is willing to look. The interesting part is that political parties do not exploit these differences as much as they could, perhaps because the positions are unsustainable (e.g., the emperors would have less bread than ever) if actually pursued in either direction to their fullest extent. Fourth, foodies and farmers have more in common than they think. Both have to eat. Both would like the opportunity to exchange goods and services in a transparent market where effort (of the farmer) and value (to the foodie) matches price, where supply meets demand, where tradeoffs (social, environmental and economic) are acknowledged, and where society eats better than it otherwise would.

Chapter 1

A View from the Barn

The central food policy in the U.S. is the *farm* bill. Any discussion of food politics must start with the politics of *farm* policy. We need a view from the barn to understand the partisan context for food policy. The barn is where farmers work and the farm is usually where farmers live. Policy has been centrally focused *on the farm* with the farm economy in mind. In short, the history of modern farm policy in the United States is essentially *the history of a social welfare policy*—a policy originally designed to prop up the incomes of farm families. Providing food for the nation was a secondary consideration. Knowing this gives us a partisan compass to navigate the anticipated roles of Republicans and Democrats in food policy. Federal social welfare policy originated with Democratic President Roosevelt's "New Deal" in 1933, and the Farm Bill is no different. Like other New Deal programs it was "an expansion of government authority" in the form of "social insurance" to "protect farmer's incomes". [1]Programs like this were *and are* a substantial plank of the Democratic Party. Programs like this are also were *and are* criticized by the Republican Party for being too costly and for distorting the "natural" workings of a free-market economy. Since social welfare policy is typically the purview of the Democratic Party, one might wonder how it is that experts in agricultural policy continually refer to it as bi-partisan or even non-partisan. This suggests the Republican Party has played a somewhat even and central role in supporting farm policy as well.

9

Why Do Farmers Need Welfare?

The rest of the book is an attempt to unravel the puzzle of "bi-partisan" support for this particular social welfare policy by exposing its *very partisan* tendencies. However, to start with we need to understand why farmers (food producers) *need* welfare in the first place, even in current times, and even if you are a small, progressive farmer. We also need to understand how this particular welfare program originated. This chapter will introduce us to the business of farming, especially the role of debt in farming and the reason farmers *might* be considered needy. This chapter will also briefly introduce the variety in agribusiness and consumer preferences.

The Business of Farming

To understand farmer's material (and thus political) concerns, it is first necessary to look at farming from the farmer's point of view. Picture the typical farm in your mind and you are likely to picture a *barn*, the quintessential symbol of the American farm. Barns are historically used to store crops and shelter livestock and machinery. Farming as a business revolves around the barn and it is a useful image for understanding commercial farming.

First, it takes capital to put food in the barn. To grow hay or grain or vegetables or fruit, one must purchase or lease land, purchase seed or saplings, obtain and apply fertilizer (manure or chemical), control pests and weeds, irrigate or hope for the right amount of rain, harvest the crop, store the crop, transport the crop to market (sometimes only once a season sometimes once a week), and, finally, contract, market or sell the crop for a price. Notice each step prior to selling takes an immense amount of money for land, machinery, supplies and labor. Putting products in the barn is not cheap! Neither it is predictable—pests, disease and weather may significantly reduce the amount in the barn in any given year. It takes a lot of luck and hard work *and capital* to put that crop in the barn. To produce poultry, pork, beef or dairy, one must feed, house, and care for livestock, also requiring inputs of hay, grain, veterinary care, land, barns, fences, etc. Fruits and vegetables are even more demanding, since they perish quickly, if not picked in a timely fashion, consumed or preserved. They also require much more water and pest control, and may also require special buildings and irrigation equipment. All of this means, more often than not, most barns are filled with borrowed money—commercial operating lines of credit (loans), mortgages, and machinery loans make that crop and livestock production possible and provide a living for all involved. This means the business of farming is usually a business in debt, and it is nothing for a relatively "small" modern family farm with an employee or two to have an operating line between $250,000 and $2 million. The end of this chapter offers some *Farmer Vignettes* to offer a view from the barn of some farmers I personally know.

Second, it takes a market to take products out of the barn. Once the barn is full, the crop mature, the livestock fattened, the eggs or the milk gathered and packaged, the farm's produce can be sold, debts repaid, and excess used for additional living expenses and capital investments. Farms typically sell their products to processors or distributors in a wholesale environment. For the grain farmer, this may mean selling to the local "elevator" who then markets and sells the grain for a small profit. For the egg farmer this means selling to the egg distributor. For the milk producer, this means selling to the milk processor. For the livestock producer, this means selling to a poultry or pork processor, usually on contract, or selling beef calves to a "backgrounder" or "finisher" generally at a local livestock auction. Progressive farms specializing in local produce or pasture-raised meat and poultry may also have wholesale (e.g., Polyface Farms) or retail (Community Supported Agriculture program, farmers markets) distribution outlets. Some of the farmers I know specialize in this type of farming and their stories can also be found in my *Farmer Vignettes* at the end of the chapter.

For many farmers, price and yield at marketing time may have great variance and uncertainty. Grain price is set by global demand since it is considered a commodity and grain yield depends a great deal on the weather—price and yield are unpredictable. Poultry, pork and specialty crops like fruits and vegetables are often grown on contract—price is predictable, but yield can vary due to pests and disease and weather. This is why there is an attraction to factory farming for pork, poultry, and eggs—even hydroponic or greenhouse vegetables!—its practices produce more predictable yields. Beef is grown for market price, but has a long investment period, with producers receiving one "crop" per year, similar to grain crops. Milk is a daily production with weekly prices set by complicated government formulas, but care of dairy livestock and replacements is year-round, and you cannot quit milking or feeding just because the weekly (or yearly!) price is down. Farmers who market their products directly can set a price, but are limited by demand and by yield quality. This means the business of farming is characterized by debt *and* instability in income.

Controlling revenue for farm products is very difficult. Because most farmers sell on a wholesale market with long-term investment and seasonal harvests, they are often at the mercy of whatever price the market gives them and whatever yields nature provides. Exacerbating the problem is the fact that they typically purchase their inputs at retail price levels, yet sell their outputs at wholesale price levels. They have a certain amount invested in their wheat or calves or milk or cucumbers, but often the price is set by global or regional conditions. The price is also set by the behavior of other farmers and the production conditions (especially weather). Furthermore, due to specialized machinery and suitable land/climate, most farmers are not that flexible year to year. They continue to grow wheat on wheat land, with wheat machinery for planting, harvest, storage and transport to market. Likewise, hay and livestock pasture is also dependent on consistent land use and machinery/capital needs (such as fencing and barns).

This also tends to make the business of agriculture slow to adjust to economic conditions and subject to boom-and-bust cycles. Farmers are especially vulnerable to over production and low prices. The boom occurs when prices are high, motivating farmers to make long-term investments in production, such as purchasing corn machinery and plowing up pasture for corn when corn prices are high; or a farmer may splurge on calves to become production cows in two years. Even vegetable or horticulture farms can suddenly ramp up to meet new farm market demands. The bust occurs when all of that new corn production or beef production or kale production or pumpkin production suddenly floods the market, lowering prices to below-profit margins. At that point it is not a good use of society's resources to re-establish pasture on corn ground or suddenly send the cow herd to a depressed market so that you do not have to feed them or to send all that kale and pumpkins to the compost pile. Society typically tries to smooth out boom-and-bust cycles, using government payments, in the name of efficient use of resources. The market has tried to smooth this out with contract growers (who have a set price ahead of time) and vertical integration (where processors contract with exclusive growers or own the animals and production facilities).

So Why Might a Farmer Be Poor?

For any given year, economists have explained the problem of low, volatile income as the result of two factors.[2] First, there is the problem of "aggregate supply and demand fundamentals". From this perspective, low and volatile pricing is caused by the fact that high yields (good weather, especially) mean plenty of supply, which leads, in the aggregate, to much lower prices. In this scenario, the farmer's income is still moderate, despite record yields, because prices are so much lower. The reverse is also true. If yields are low (perhaps again due to weather) prices will be higher, but the farmer has much less to sell, again resulting in moderate income.

A second problem is the long production time for seasonal crops and livestock. The farmer cannot quickly ramp up production when prices are high or rapidly reduce production when prices are low. Sunk costs are already present in crop seed, fertilizer, and land use—and the season might be too well advanced to plow it up and plant something else. Likewise, sunk costs are already present in feeding and caring for livestock or tending vegetables, and if they are not sold at peak readiness, quality suffers and costs such as feeding or storage or spoilage mount while waiting for a more favorable market. Furthermore, all farmers in an area use the same growing season, so their products arrive at the market at the same time, usually out-pacing demand temporarily, but with the effect of lowering prices. It is even possible for a farmer to appear prosperous—land, machinery, new pick-up truck—and still clear only a few thousand a year after expenses. In

Rockbridge County, Virginia, where I live, the 2012 USDA average farm income was $2000 a year.

How Can They Compete?

Farmers can compete a few ways. They can "store" their crops, until prices rise, but that takes money—whether building a bin, renting storage from a co-op, or feeding calves to maintain them. Some crops, such as vegetables and milk do not store well. Farmers can also use sophisticated marketing tools, such as forward contracting, to sell their crops ahead of time. The risk is that yield is unknown, and farmers are never sure if they will have the product to fulfill the contract. For this reason, farmers may also buy insurance for at least a portion of their crop. Most grain farmers have 65-85% of their crop insured for weather damage. Most livestock producers have 10-15% of their herd insured for deaths or losses. Newer federal farm programs have created insurance for hay and vegetables. Farmers also seek out production methods to minimize risk, such as investing in irrigation or greenhouses or large factory-like livestock facilities (to control risk from pests, weather, cannibalism, etc.). Farmers who sell directly to consumers have different challenges, usually meeting demand or overproducing for the market. Imagine how much farm produce is not purchased at a farmers market and is actually taken back to the farm to become compost. Quality, too, can affect retail sales. While most large direct-sale farms have access to processors for less-than-supermarket quality fruits and vegetables (e.g., bruised apples for applesauce, ripened tomatoes for pasta sauce), small producers might not have sufficient scale to do so. Their "ugly" produce may go to waste.

Strategies for farm production can be quite varied, but typically follow patterns. Grain farmers store and use forward contract, hedge and "put" marketing strategies. Livestock and milk producers sell according to market conditions when product is ready (you cannot store fat calves or milk) or may contract ahead of time. Vegetable and fruit growers contract to wholesalers and processors using seasonal market prices and contract production, with a small portion of the market using direct retail sales. In all instances, however, there is an asymmetry in the rhythms of producing versus selling.

Needy Farmers

The social welfare problem in farming arises when market prices are lower than production prices, leaving the farmer in the red despite a year's hard work. This typically occurs when production outstrips demand, lowering prices. It can also arise when weather or disease significantly wipes out or reduces a crop's quality and quantity. Exacerbating the problem is the reality and perception that middle men reap large profits on the shipping and processing and retailing of food stuffs.

So How Can Government Help?

From the farmers' perspective, there are five ways government policy can contribute directly to the prospects in the barn: (1) subside research and development to make farms more efficient, (2) stabilize credit availability, (3) offer subsidized insurance to manage risk, (4) open new markets through trade or domestic nutrition programs (SNAP farmer's markets, Farm-to School), and (5) direct market intervention in the form of production controls or farm subsidies.[3] The goal of these interventions is to increase farm viability—to make the farm economically sustainable. From the perspective of larger society, modern "interventionist" government also uses farm policy to pursue other goals: health and nutrition, rural development, and regulation of agribusiness on multiple levels, such as with environmental or labor/occupational rules.

Political Farming

The business of farming thus anticipates the political demands of farmers. With a their need for capital, most farmers are debtors—and this has historically made them intensely interested in monetary policy, the regulation of banks, the printing of money and interest rates. This also means that farmers are not necessarily the friends of capitalists and "big business". With a need for income stability (in a volatile market environment), farmers are essentially welfare recipients—and this has historically meant that farmers have demanded subsidized incomes from government, in one form or another—price support, market controls, subsidies, and insurance products. This also means that farmers are not necessarily friends with consumers or taxpayers, who must live in a food economy with higher prices or higher taxes. That said, farmers, as a welfare class, have enjoyed strong political support due to their historical numbers and to their privileged and symbolic status in American culture.

Know Your Farm Lobby: Part Republican, Part Democrat

At this point, it might also make sense to introduce the political history of farmer-based lobby groups, especially the American Farm Bureau Federation, the Grange and the National Farmers Union—all active federated groups today with chapters in most Congressional districts. Early in the 1900's the government sought to assist farmers with education and technology by extending the work of the land grant colleges to the countryside using "extension agents." These extension agents formed local farm organizations modeled on the chamber of commerce—a place where farmers could obtain educational/technical help with the "business" of farming. Originally serving as educational and social outlets organized by the

USDA, these "county farm bureaus" quickly realized their potential for grassroots political action and organization. Formally organized as a federation in 1919, The American Farm Bureau Federation galvanized its membership, and took its political concerns to Congress with smashing results. Unexpectedly, a Republican-led "Farm Bloc" defied party leadership and passed six bills to assist farmers with middle-men and credit—regulating packers, milk distributors, and grain exchanges as well as extending the wartime farm loan program—all in one year, 1921. Notice these were *Republican* Senators—*against* party leadership. Democrats are the ones who are usually pursuing these types of "progressive" measures to level the playing field. So why Republicans? These were *Midwest* Republicans facing organized Farm Bureaus back home. As we will see, parochial (local) politics in farm policy will create strange bedfellows—like Republicans pushing for progressive (Democratic!) reforms.

The American Farm Bureau Federation (AFBF) was not the only farm lobby group to have significant membership at this time. The Grange movement was a more militant group with fraternal rituals, somewhat limiting its membership. However, even today, the Grange movement is active as a farmer and rural youth social and political organization. The National Farmers Union, also still active today, supported the most radical populist demands of farmers, with significant regional standing among wheat farmers in the prairie and cotton growers in the south. Today the NFU stands for unionized farm labor and heavy farm subsidies and supports. Over time, the NFU became associated with the Democratic Party and the AFB with the Republican Party. However, the AFBF had exceptional organizational strength as a federation, with decentralized, yet organized constituency, allowing it to dominate Congressional Agricultural Committees.[4] Because it is national in scope and membership, the Bureau was also the best situated to facilitate legislative vote-trading among the farm regions and their representatives when designing farm policy in Congress. In contemporary times, AFB advocates for market-based solutions rather than subsidies, price controls or tariffs, putting them closer to Republican goals.

Modern party coalitions do not map neatly onto the needs of these farm groups, and the history of American farm and food politics demonstrates more conflicting interests than uniform interests, mostly due to the dominance of economic values in farm policy. Furthermore, scholars agree that what started as agrarian populism and "general" farm organizational lobbying (AFB especially) has devolved into commodity and producer organizations (Wheat, Corn, Cotton, Beef, Organic Growers, etc.) who practice "clientele" politics with their patrons on the Agricultural Committees in Congress to obtain narrow, yet favorable treatment in the Farm Bill. These groups tend to be business organizations, but with a business which is often geographically-based, retaining some of the parochial (local) tendencies. According to political scientist Grant McConnell, Mid-twentieth century farm policy conflicts tended to be resolved by deals cut by committed House and Senate members cooperating with private commodity organizations and supported by local farm industries.[5]

Know Your Farmer: One Size Does Not Fit All

Contemporary treatments of agriculture tend to lump all industrialized farming and agribusiness into a monolithic corporate group, usually with the accusation that they dominate politics to the detriment of other societal interests. However, a carful treatment of farm and food politics should understand that government "help" is nuanced and decentralized precisely because of the cross pressures of a nuanced and decentralized food production system.

Political parties are coalitions of interests, which organize to obtain favorable policies. However, when it comes to farmers, agribusiness and food processors, these three groups have different priorities and incentives, meaning that they will not necessarily favor *the same* policies. Furthermore, each group is not monolithic. Programs for wheat farmers are different than programs for dairy farmers. The needs of the grain farmer for higher returns on their crops necessarily limits the profitability of the livestock farmers (beef, poultry, pork and dairy) use grain as a input and desire it to be cheap. Progressive organic farmers and conventional commodity farmers may also find themselves on opposite sides of policy debates, as will manufacturing processors and farmers who disagree whether almonds or soy are "milk" or cattlemen who lament lab-grown "meat."

Agri-business, too, is not monolithic. Do we mean grain buyers and processors, such as Archer Daniels Midland, which produces corn syrup and oilseed products, or Perdue Farms, which produces poultry fattened on grain? Or, do we mean Bayer (formerly Monsanto), who sells grain inputs (seed and chemicals) to farmers? ADM and Perdue necessarily want to promote lower grain prices, so they can purchase corn and soybeans at the lowest possible price. Bayer wants profitable farmers who can afford to purchase the latest seed and chemical technology for their fields. Additional market players, such as farm equipment manufacturers, bank lenders and grocers and restaurants have different incentives in the process. Contemporary writings too often lump all of these varied interests together, especially when the grocer is Kroger and the restaurant is McDonalds, and political history often lamented the powerful "farm bloc" as all of these working against the interests of "the people." However, as we will see, these differences provide openings for political parties competing for votes and electoral support by offering to support a variable menu of farm and food programs.

Know Your Foodie: A View from the Grocery Aisle and the Corner Cafe

Complicating the politics even more are the food consumers, yet another group that has incredible variety, and considerable attraction for partisans looking to attract votes. Contemporary consumers may want cheap food *or* fine food, convenient food *or* slow food, comfort food *or* healthy food, sensual food *or* moral food. They want food retailers to cater to their every whim and taste—whether at a grocery store or at a restaurant.

Yet, urban dwellers need farmers.

When Aristotle explored what made the best city, his list included farmers because "cities need farmers to provide for the necessities of life."[6] Economists Norwood and Lusk echo this sentiment in their observation that "virtually everything we consume is produced by other people" and "Agriculture allowed and perhaps caused humans to live in densely populated areas"[7] That said, farm and consumer interests do not necessarily align. During New Deal politics in the 1930's, the government sought to control farm prices by heavily regulating farm production in such policies as the American Agricultural Adjustment Act, the first real Farm Bill. Historically, government designed these programs to control supply so that farmers could reap a better price for staples such as wheat and dairy. However, that also had the effect of raising the prices for food, such as bread and butter. Thus, what benefits the farmer did not necessarily benefit the consumer, creating interesting problems for a government catering to both. It is even more complicated when one considers that over one-third of New Deal consumers *were farmers* too!

Furthermore, blessed by American food abundance, modern consumers have had the luxury of pursing other food values beyond economics—and these were not necessarily farmer friendly if they added to the cost of production. For the "first generation" foodie, values were, like farm economics, *material* values, such as food safety, animal heath, or environmental pollution. These consumer interests resulted in meat packing laws, pesticide residue restrictions, and animal welfare requirements. To be fair to farmers, most of them likewise value food safety, animal well-being and sustainable farms—because these values are vital to their business. For the very contemporary foodie, *moral* values, such as food democracy, social justice or local promotion also come into play. Contemporary consumers often pursue policies about food labeling, healthy food access, sustainability, and even more "humane" animal production models, such as cage-free or free-range mandates. Helping them along are pioneering chefs and grocery outlets seeking to carve out special markets with special social values. While spurring new farm innovations and markets, these political demands have also increased the regulatory burden on food producers, even for small, progressive farmers and specialty chefs, increasing the "price" of food production.

Of course, other consumers are just worried about putting food on the table, with little *luxury* for politics. Advocates for the needs of these consumers support free choice in government grocery dollars, food banks and food charity programs, and realistic nutrition programming, such as doubling farm market dollars for SNAP beneficiaries. Like farmers, these consumers and their advocates are concerned about the economics of food policy.

A View from the Voting Booth?

Each of these concerns has interesting implications for partisan politics as Democrats and Republicans take sides in the policy debate. As noted above, Democrats historically support social welfare programs. In recent years, they also have carved out a place supporting many foodie issues, including progressive concerns about food safety and animal welfare and post-material concerns about the environment, poverty and social justice. By contrast, Republicans generally enjoy political support from rural, traditionally minded areas, especially on cultural issues, yet seem to be moving away from supporting farm welfare programs. Reflecting greater overall ideology Republican tend to support as free a market as possible, even for raw milk, farm market vegetables and hemp. Don't these differences imply partisan, even polarized, approaches to farm policy? If so, how is it that experts still view food policy as bipartisan? Furthermore, what do these differences mean for food politics in the voting booth? How do parties compete for farmer and foodie votes?

Farmer Vignettes: A View from the Barn

Did you have diary, grain, poultry, beef or vegetables this week? Step into the barn and meet a few farmers I know.

Spring Branch Dairy, Virginia

A young brother-sister partnership, oversees a modest dairy of 250 Holsteins in the Shenandoah Valley. The three-generation dairy recently celebrated 50 years. Sister is the herdswoman, managing all milk operations and dairy care, with the help of two milking robots. Brother is the crop farmer, managing the alfalfa, corn, soybeans and hay that supply foodstuffs for the cows and some cash crops. A full-time employee helps both (with additional part-time help in the summer). Though nearing retirement, Mom and Dad also help. Mom manages the dairy calves and helps with hauling crops and parts runs. Dad assists with the crop harvests and mechanics. Like most dairies, Spring Branch dairy is dependent on milk prices and grain prices for its annual income, on herd health for milk production, and on weather for herd and crop production. The milk truck comes several times a week to pick up milk for the processor. According to Sister, milk prices need to be at $18 or $19 to make the farm profitable. The milk price in 2019 is at $17 per hundred pounds of milk with a government formula, but it was $14 for two years before that. This made operation loans, building loans and other expenses difficult to maintain, and the family has often worked for very little return or even a loss some months. According to *Lancaster Farming*, a prominent Mid-Atlantic diary news source, suicides and other social problems have arisen on cash-strapped dairy farms in 2019. Diary prices are suffering from a reduced American demand for dairy products, and only the largest diaries, such as Three-Mile Canyon in Oregon (A Tillamook Diary with 25,000 cows) or Fair Oaks (Northern Indiana near Chicago, milking 30,000 cows) have the marginal rates of return and corporate vertical structure to make diary profitable. In the case of Spring Branch Diary, we see a family who has built their farm for generations (and cultivated a high-producing herd) and who cannot imagine just selling out to go work in town, so they keep milking, planting, feeding, caring, and producing, even when prices are below cost or unsustainable long-term. The farm has also sought to diversify to cash crop production to improve economic conditions, and the farm participates in USDA commodity subsidy programs and crop insurance programs.

Rancho Arroyo, Texas

This small 35-acre irrigated farm three miles from the border in South Texas, is home to a family of six, with mother and grandmother as the farm's primary managers. Rancho Arroyo received a grant from USDA to upgrade its aging irrigation to maintain a pasture-raised poultry operation with direct sales to restaurants and farm market customers. However, after only a few years, the farm struggled to find a large enough local market for its expensive poultry, and was forced to convert the land to hay production. When hay prices fell, even the hay did not meet the expenses of watering and fertilizing it. Today the land is rented by a larger farming operation for a small payment, the pasture fed poultry, pork and beef is gone, and the "farmers" have retired or found off-farm work.

Bear Mountain Ranch, Oregon

This 750-acre farm in Central Oregon had seven irrigation pivots and supported two families—one for the farmer and one for the hired man. The farm also relied on seasonal migrant labor to assist with production. At its peak, this farm produced several profitable crops for retail and contract, including square-bale horse hay, seed garlic/wheat/grass for contract, mint for distilleries, wholesale potatoes, sugar beets under contract and a few head of beef for the family. Because the farm was in a high desert, weather was steady and water was purchased via water rights from the local irrigation district. In fact, the owner served as President of his irrigation board in the 1990's and oversaw dam repairs for the valley. At its peak, the ranch used a $250,000 operating line to provide payroll and farm expenses. The farm's ability to modify the weather risk and maximize production with irrigation made this a profitable, economically sustainable farm. The farmer's family lived on a modest $40,000 or less income per year, but managed a middle-class lifestyle, and did not participate in USDA programs or subsidies. The farm has since changed hands to a lifestyle beef and hay operation, and the small community has been taken over by retirees and recent Google and Facebook server installations seeking dry, consistent climate. Availability of water, high labor costs, loss of markets for sugar beets, horse hay, garlic, mint and other crops forced the family to reinvest in Illinois farm ground growing corn & soybeans.

Shiloh Farms, Illinois

This 2500-acre corn & soybean farm is owned and managed by a father/son team who also own and manage a small real estate office in Central Illinois. Three-fourths of the ground is rented or farmed on shares, and is located within a 25 mile radius of the Archer Daniels Midland plant in Decatur, Illinois. Farm season is about six weeks in Spring for planting and six weeks in Fall for harvest, freeing up labor for the family's real estate business. Two part-time employees help with the farm. The family markets their grain to elevators owned by ADM and by a small competitor, Top Flight Grain. In the past, farmer's co-ops owned the small elevators five or ten miles apart, sometimes having eight or ten in the county. The facilities are still there, receiving grain at harvest, but all of them have been bought out by ADM or Top Flight. Tate and Lyle, another large grain processor, also has a plant in Decatur, and many farmers market there, as well. In recent years, University of Illinois has put break-even corn & soybean prices above what most farmers can obtain at elevator harvest prices. Revenue insurance, subsidized by the federal farm bill, provides the opportunity to insure up to 85% of the crop, allowing the family to aggressively forward contract their grain during the off-season, when prices are higher. If the weather or prices change, the insurance is there to back them up, so that they are sure to fulfill their contracts one way or the other. This type of insurance is based on historic yields, making it very lucrative in a high-producing area such as Central Illinois. (By contrast, a farmer in Virginia, where I call home, would have a hard time insuring acreage for high-yielding corn without a supportive ten-year production history—something much less likely in the Mid-Atlantic climate. Thus, a Shenandoah Valley producer can only insure up to 65% of the county average—even though production for a particular year might have been higher. There are farmers who have gotten 75-bushel beans in a county with 35-bushel average, allowing for insurance on only 22-bushels per acre. This makes it difficult to pre-market more than 22 of those bushels ahead of time, leaving the farmer with much lower price at harvest.)

McElwee Farm, Virginia

Two brothers and an elderly mother manage a beef & turkey farm. Turkey has been commercially grown in the Shenandoah Valley since before the Civil War. Originally the birds were raised in outdoor flocks and herded on roads to market. In modern times, commercial turkeys are grown in large, technologically monitored barns. This farm grows Turkeys for Cargill in two large Turkey Barns, housing 18,000 birds each, and they grow hay, corn for silage to feed the cattle on their 150-acre farm. The brothers built Turkey barns, now worth about $1 million each, on contract from Cargill. They receive poults (baby turkeys) from Cargill and a feed truck from Cargill's local plant visits weekly to supply the feed. The brothers are paid a contract pound price when the turkeys are full-grown and loaded into a truck after 20 weeks. The brothers grow several flocks of turkeys within a year's time. Their biggest risk is a disease outbreak, such as Bird Flu, which could destroy a flock overnight. They also have to keep the Turkey's at peak temperatures, making weather and long power-outages a problem.

Waddell Farm, Virginia

This farm is 176-acres of alternating corn and soybeans in the Shenandoah Valley. A Husband-Wife team farms together, using off farm income from the wife's professional job for working capital. The wife does the seed selection, planting and marketing of the crop, as well as various tractor work during harvest. Her farmer-partner husband does the mechanic work and the harvesting with a 25-year-old John Deere combine and trucks the grain himself to a local poultry co-op owned by Mennonite farmers. Like many production farms in the Shenandoah Valley, the farm uses cover crops and riparian zones to protect the Chesapeake Bay from sediment and nitrogen. The farm dedicated two acres to vegetable production with natural methods for a time, producing sweet corn, snap peas, cucumbers, watermelons and pumpkins using drip irrigation, hand cultivation techniques, and no pesticides. These products were sold wholesale at a Mennonite Produce Auction and retail through a farm stand and a local healthy foods co-op. Farm stand prices covered costs except for labor. The farm also sells premium orchard grass hay in small square bales to local horse, sheep, goat farms, and supports a small herd of cattle (and calves) on upland meadows, using manure in farm production. Both husband and wife manage the hay and cattle. Waddell Farm operates without USDA farm subsidies and uses off-farm income (rather than operating loans) to provide working capital for the farm. Major crops are profitable for the farm, using only family labor. The USDA would classify Waddell farm as a "residential-lifestyle farm" a category encompassing 50% of American farms including cattle, timber, horses, grain, horticulture, vegetable and Christmas tree farms. Unlike Waddell farm, many of these farms do take advantage of USDA-backed insurance, commodity subsidies, specialty farm grants, and conservation payments and cost-shares. Farmers contribute a small amount to the food, fiber and horticulture supply in return for these government programs.

Polyface Contractor, Rockbridge County, Virginia

Living on 20 acres this farm is primarily run by a professional woman with day job in town. She and her father grow beef, chicken and eggs to be marketed through Polyface Farms in Swoope, Virgina. Like other contractors nearby, the farm is distinctive for its daily rotation (movement) of cattle and range chickens in the pasture. Polyface contractors are usually small and easily distinguished from the conventional farms nearby. The cows are concentrated in large groups on small plots. The chickens are not in warehouses, but roam in small moving pastures with a mobile roof nearby. The farms may be less tidy in appearance, particularly due to their tolerance for weeds, their poly-species pastures—both plant and animal form. They are also less capital intensive with small, simple machinery needs—no large barns or tractors here.

Shenandoah Meats

This Farm Family has farmed in Rockbridge County for over 200 years. While the daughter went to Virginia Tech and has an established career in commercial farm production and agronomics, the son went straight to the land, farming cattle and grain. All family members are still involved in the family farm. In order to diversify the farm, the son and his Dad retail their own meat through farmers markets, restaurants and a family-owned butcher shop. Very recently, they made local news as the first large scale hemp farm working with Virginia Tech to develop hemp in Virginia. Hemp is a frontier for farmers, even in terms of growing, obtaining seeds or starts, regulation, processing and retail. Land Grant universities are playing catch up to create research and support for this new CBD oil industry.

---

[1] Adam Sheingate, *The Rise of the Agricultural Welfare State* (Princeton, NJ: Princeton University Press, 2001), p. 1.

[2] James Novak et al., *Agricultural Policy in the United States* (New York: Routledge, 2015), p. 2.

[3] Economists offer a much longer, technical list of government interventions to affect supply and demand: price supports, input subsidies, income subsidies (for both farmer or consumer), production subsidies, and marketing controls. Novak et al. p. 18.

[4] McConnell, Grant. *Private Power and American Democracy.* (New York: Alfred A. Knopf, 1966) Chapter 7.

[5] McConnell, Grant. *Private Power and American Democracy.* (New York: Alfred A. Knopf, 1966) Chapter 7

[6] Aristotle, Book IV

[7] Norwood, F. Bailey, and Jayson Lusk. *Compassion by the Pound: The Economics of Farm Animal Welfare.* (Oxford: Oxford University Press, 2011) p. 17.

Chapter 2

The Sport of Team Politics

Voting with our fork requires us to realize that voting in America usually means choosing between a Democratic or Republican candidate for office. So what do we know about Democrats and Republicans? We know they are considered the dominate teams in American Politics. But what does that mean—and how can it help us understand food politics better?

I have found that a sports analogy works best for me when I am thinking about the way the experts see political parties. The easiest way to discuss political parties is to *really think about* them as teams. They have team colors, nicknames and mascots. They have players, positions, stats. They even have rotating stadium locations (Conventions anyone?) and tournaments, which the pundits call "presidential and midterm" elections. Political parties have a loyal fan base, star players and even coaches. And of course, political parties want to score political goals by working as a team to pass their preferred policy. But what do we know about these teams? Who is on each team (and who are their fans in the stands)? When did these teams form? How have they changed? How do they play the game? What is their win-loss record? To understand political parties and food, we have to understand the game of team politics.

Red Team, Blue Team

While most readers are likely familiar with the teams, here is a brief recap of where things stand in the American Political League. The red team is the Republican Party. Its nickname is the Grand Old Party, and its mascot is the elephant. The Republican team today tends to dominate rural areas and so called "heartland" states in the middle of the nation. As the party of Abraham Lincoln, winner of the Civil War, the Republican team dominated American politics from 1860-1896 and 1900-1932. They enjoyed a resurgence in 1952 (President Eisenhower), 1980 (President Reagan), 1994 (Speaker Newt Gingrich), 2002 (9/11), 2010 (House Tea Party) and 2016 (President Trump). Historically they suffered from a player scandal in the 1970's (Nixon's Watergate) and from losing foreign policy strategies such as Vietnam and the Iraq War. The Republican team's coalition of interests includes corporate free-market interests, fiscal conservatives, gun rights, and evangelicals.

The blue team is the Democratic Party. Its mascot is the donkey. The Democratic team today tends to dominate the Northeast and the West Coast, along with most metropolitan areas including small manufacturing or university towns. As the party of the progressives and Franklin Delano Roosevelt, the Democratic team dominated American politics from 1932-1964 and controlled the House from 1964-1994. It enjoyed a resurgence in 1992 (Clinton) and 2008 (Obama) and 2018 (Speaker Pelosi and colleagues). Historically, their political support suffered from their association with the counterculture in the 1960s and 1970s and from their association with the controversial social welfare policies in the Great Society and Obamacare. The Democratic team's coalition of interests includes unions, minorities, feminists, immigrants, environmentalists, and the LGBT community.

According to political scientists, the main differences between the red team and the blue team have to do with New Deal and minority politics.[1] The blue team, Democrats, believe in the use of government to solve society's problems, especially social problems, such as poverty or racism. To accomplish this, Democratic Party passed a multitude of New Deal economic and social programs in the 1930's and pursued civil rights and anti-poverty programs in the 1960's. By contrast, Republicans are skeptical of government's ability to generate wealth or liberty, something they feel the free-market and a free nation offers to all who work hard. Since 1932, Republicans have largely resisted New Deal economic and social agendas, and have been reluctant to adopt additional regulations on states and firms in the name of equality. The expansion of government has been promoted by one and resisted by the other fairly consistently in modern politics, with exception of law enforcement and national security (where Republicans tend to support more expansive government power and spending). As we shall see, these game plans have had a very real impact on farm & food policy.

Players

Like any team, political parties have players, coaches and fans. The players have important positions with key responsibilities. The players wear the jersey and move the ball down the field. In politics, the positions are usually well known, even if names are not.

Legislators

Legislators pass laws. These are members of the House of Representatives, Senators, and their counterparts in state legislatures. They are typically elected by geographically defined districts, and they serve for a certain length of time. Most importantly for our purposes, the members of the House of Representatives are re-elected every two years, infusing the federal government with a fresh agenda on a regular basis. Senators are re-elected every six years, with staggered terms, so that only one-third of the Senate turns over at a time.

The terms of service have important implications for food policy. The House, because of its frequent election, is closest to the whims of the people. This means most policy passed by the House is generally more extreme or dramatic, swinging with shifts in opinion. By contrast, the Senate has fewer fresh faces and less spur-of-the-moment zeal, so its policy tends to be more moderate and incremental. This can easily be seen in the House and Senate approaches to the Farm Bill in 2014, as discussed in the introduction. The House bill had much more dramatic changes to nutrition (food stamp) spending and commodity subsidies than the Senate version. At the state level, legislators tend to work on a smaller and more localized scale, often with an even keener sense of what their voters want. For this reason, states can be more creative and experimental in their policy, pioneering innovative approaches to food or farm policy. For example, in recent years states have pioneered labeling genetically modified food, regulating raw milk sales, accepting SNAP benefits at farmer's markets, protecting farmers' "freedom to farm" and providing immunity to fast food chains in obesity law suits.

Legislators operate in a *majority* rules environment, so they have to coordinate their efforts *as a team* in order to implement their agenda. In the House, with its 435 members, this coordination can take a top-down approach. Leaders of the chamber (Speaker of the House, Majority Leader, Minority Leader, etc.) lay out an agenda for their party and use their authority to enforce "team" discipline. Rank-in-file members are pressured to help move the ball down the field or risk losing committee positions, campaign assistance, or chamber support for policies *they* want to move forward.

Juxtaposed to the chamber leadership are committee chairs, who oversee the development of bills within their committee's part of the field. In food policy, the most important committees are the House Agricultural Committee and the House Appropriations Committee. While the appropriations committee (which votes to spend the money) tends to be more closely aligned with party leaders, the Agricultural Committee has often been at odds with the stated agenda of party leaders at the top of the House hierarchy. Most notably this conflict between committee chairs and chamber leadership occurs when the Republican team wants to cut government spending or wants to tinker less with free market forces in Agriculture. However, the House Agriculture members are more committed to protecting the needs of farmers, and they will often work hard to protect subsidies or other programs from the chopping block, even if they are Republican. On the Democratic side, while party leadership may wish to limit farm subsidies to so called "wealthy" farmers or may seek stricter environmental regulations for farmers, Democrats from farm districts or on the House Ag committee may work to moderate these tendencies.

The Senate, with only 100 members, works quite differently. Because Senators by tradition and rules can *individually* hold up legislation in a variety of tactics, most Senate work requires unanimous consent or super-majority cooperation (60 votes) to pass legislation. Party leaders have much less power over individual Senators, and any member can cause policy work to come to a standstill. Because so many members must agree, Senate legislation tends to be much more moderate or much more loaded with narrow, individualized wish lists (called "pork") to gain the votes of most members. Compared to the House, at least, policymaking in the Senate tends toward smaller changes, so as to threaten no member's principles or material concerns too much, such as offering a slight reduction in food stamp spending. As for specific pork provisions, members from states with niche agriculture, such as salmon fishing or exotic timber or tropical fruit or wool production, will seek extra provisions to benefit their local industries.

Presidents and Other Executives

Presidents are the most well-known player on any political team, and they are often perceived as opinion leaders for their party. If the President lays out an agenda, party leaders in Congress usually get behind at least part of it, even with very controversial presidents, such as Donald Trump. Presidents are chiefly responsible for organizing and leading a team to implement the laws of Congress. Presidents appoint their Cabinet members to oversee policy implementation in the various executive departments, with the most important being Secretary of State (international diplomacy), Secretary of Treasury (collecting & spending money) and the Attorney General (enforcing the law). In the case of food and agriculture, the leadership of the USDA (farming and nutrition), the EPA (environment) and the Department of Commerce are key players, as well as the US Trade Representative. Historically, the President's most forceful food policy appointment was the Secretary of Agriculture, who would set the tone for food production in the United States. The Secretary of Agriculture oversees a variety of federal programs including supplemental nutrition (SNAP), food safety, school lunch, conservation programs and commodity programs, and the department historically implemented strict farm production regulations. Other agencies also play a role in farm and ranch policy. For example, the Bureau of Land Management and the Bureau of Reclamation, in the Department of the Interior, regulate grazing, water rights and irrigation. The individuals who manage federal programs, at the behest of the president, wield significant influence on food policy because *they make the rules*. Whether it is an EPA rule about pesticides or a

USDA rule about organic production or an FDA rule about food labeling, Congress gives agencies broad authority to make specific rules *for firms and individuals to follow*, including those who grow, eat, sell, manufacture or prepare food.

Presidents, with the help of their accountants and economists at the Office of Management and Budget (The presidential administration's accountants & economists), also monitor government spending and budget requirements. While Congress controls the purse, the annual budget process starts with the president's presentation of the budget to Congress, which is generally perceived as the administration's most forceful policy statement. To see a president's priorities, just look at the administration's proposed budget. Some of the more interesting conflicts in American food policy have surfaced as budget issues. For example, President George W. Bush famously vetoed the 2002 Farm Bill over spending concerns, only to be overruled by Congress with *Republican* support.

Presidents also take the lead on international policy. As the face of America to the rest of the world, Presidents and their staff are given the task of negotiating trade treaties with other nations. President Clinton negotiated the North American Free Trade Agreement (NAFTA), which opened up export markets for US corn to Mexico and US dairy to Canada. The same agreement allowed for the import of Mexican sugar and Canadian fertilizer to the U.S. President Obama negotiated the Trans-Pacific Partnership, in part to open Asian markets, particularly Japan, to even more U.S. agricultural goods. Both NAFTA and TPP were negated by President Trump who sought to negotiate his own trade agreements, disrupting longstanding American agricultural export and farm production models.

Finally, as mentioned above, presidents are opinion leaders sometimes setting the tone for generation. Their statements on food or farming policy can make a lasting impression on other players and on voters. And, the system often moves in the direction of a presidential agenda. During the 1920's, President Calvin Coolidge vetoed farm assistance programs passed by Congress, setting a tone for Republican Party aversion to New Deal farm programs a decade later. President Ronald Reagan famously spoke of the wasteful farm programs in a 1964 speech (yes, before he was even President) which galvanized Republican deficit hawks. First Lady, Michelle Obama, used her White House lawn to promote healthy eating and exercise for the nation's youth and also worked to obtain the passage of the Healthy Hunger-Free Kids program of 2010.

At the state level, governors oversee state program implementation. State departments of agriculture supply a range of farm services and promotional work. State-level trade agencies will often promote state agricultural goods to the rest of the world in a variety of ways—hosting trade trips, facilitating industry growth in foreign markets, quality control, etc. States also regulate farming and food production in unique ways to promote local values.

Judges

Judges are often regarded as referees in politics keeping the other policymaking players within the rules and interpreting the law. However, most political observers understand that judges are human and likely have favorites and principles they generally support in their judging. Most judges do not wear red or blue jerseys—at least not officially. Judicial offices tend to be non-partisan, even at the state level, hence the *regulation black robe* uniform to symbolize impartiality.

Party in Government

Political scientists refer to red and blue players as the Party in Government. Morris Fiorina wrote an influential scholarly article lamenting the decline of party (team) discipline in the ranks of Congress.[2] He felt that individuals in Congress, especially committee chairs and Senators had too much power to *act independently*, weakening the ability of the party to work together as a team and move a particular policy "ball" down the field. Presidential scholars, too, have lamented the inability of the President to implement a *partisan* agenda. Richard Neustadt famously said a President has to have the "power to persuade" because he cannot make law (Congress does) and because he is not the only leader of the executive branch.[3] Neustadt noted that executive agencies also answer to Congress (who funds them, authorizes them, creates them, investigates them, etc.), clients (such as farmers or food companies), and their career staff (such as line meat inspectors, nutrition scientists, local conservation officials, etc.), giving them some independence of the President. For this reason, many scholars have considered political parties *weak* operators on the individual prerogatives of members of Congress, presidents or executive branch bureaucrats.

However, things seemed to have changed in recent years. In 1994, Congress enacted a series of reforms within its House chamber to reconsolidate power back to the Speaker and party leaders. Committee chairs had become too powerful and the new rules basically meant chairs would serve at the pleasure of the Speaker rather than according to seniority alone. Other measures of party discipline were also created, having the effect of making rank-in-file members at least somewhat submissive to party leadership. This has allowed Republicans and Democrats of recent years the ability to pursue *much more* partisan agendas when they control the chamber—most notably with the Republicans after 1994 (Speaker Newt Gingrich), 2002 (Speaker Dennis Hastert), 2016 (Speaker Paul Ryan) and with the Democrats (Speaker Nancy Pelosi) after 2006 and 2008 and again with Democratic Progressives in 2019.

Team Unity?

Even more importantly than team rules has been the emergence of team unity, particularly *ideological* (conservative or liberal) over the decades. Historically, Republicans since the Civil War typically hailed from the Northeast, the Midwest, and the Northwest. As might be expected, these fellow partisans had quite different views of how the world worked or should work. Republicans from places like New York had much more cosmopolitan and liberal views of the world than those from Missouri, for example, who tended to be more provincial and conservative in their views. Northwestern Republicans were even more different, with a frontier ethic of independence and openness. Likewise, historically, Democrats since the Civil War typically hailed from the South (Anti-Lincoln) and the urban industrial centers, where progressive and labor interests were strong. Southern Democrats tended to be very conservative in their views, while Northern Democrats pursued a much more progressive agenda.

Are We Even on the Same Team?

Prior to 1968, when Richard Nixon was first elected, each party was a regionally varied mix of partisans which often meant that team members could not always be counted on to move a partisan ball forward, and more often than not, might even run the ball the other way! Democrats had trouble with their Southern members cooperating with Republicans on rural and conservative matters. Republicans had trouble with their New England members often cooperating with Democrats on urban and progressive matters. This tendency for cross-team coalitions meant that farm policy and food policy would often have odd mixes of Republican and Democratic support, depending on the particulars of a policy. In other words, for roughly a century after the Civil War, the two parties had a *mix* of ideologies and many more *moderates* in their ranks in Congress.

However, all of this began to change starting in the 1960's. The Democratic Party opened itself up to a civil rights agenda, which put it at odds with Southern segregationist Democrats. The Republican Party also reiterated its commitment to free market economics and increasingly courted conservative evangelicals. This shift alienated many of the more liberal New England Republicans. It also had the effect of eventually delivering the conservative South into the Red team and the liberal Northeast into the Blue team. Moderates who did not tow party lines of conservatism or liberalism found it increasingly difficult to fit into their respective parties.

Great Minds, Thinking Alike

Today's two major parties are much more ideologically cohesive—typically agreeing on a liberal or conservative agenda in principle and working together as a team to achieve it in practice. This also means that players on the two opposing teams tend to be poles apart, with little agreement on middle ground. Since legislation generally requires at least some cooperation, particularly in the Senate, this has the unsatisfying effect of making legislation a watered down or cobbled together affair no single party can genuinely get behind, even if they claim it. The Affordable Care Act of 2010, a Democratic law, had little for progressive Democrats to cheer about, since it continued to give the free market at least some role in American health care, rather than a single-payer, Medicare-for-all model. Likewise the Republican tax reform of 2017 did not enact near the level of tax-reform on a conservative wish-list. Farm bills, too, are notoriously "catch-all" in their nature, to allow most Representatives and Senators at least something to be happy about, whether deficit reduction or programs for minority farmers, both of which were part of the 2014 farm bill.

Scholars have found this new ideological unity to be a mixed bag for democracy. On the one hand, voters have clear choices among the parties and they know who to hold responsible for many "failed" policies. This is the type of "responsible party government" yearned for by Morris Fiorina—voters can hold parties responsible. However, other scholars are worried about the inability to govern when parties are poles apart in a constitutional system that requires compromise and cooperation to get things done. Nicol Rae warned the Fiorina-types to "be careful what you wish for."[4] Parties which are unified and able to police their players can enact somewhat dramatic agendas when they have the Congress and the presidency. But when government is divided, and when parties committed to very separate and polarized agendas, the system can descend into a chaos where the parties never agree to govern at all—leaving pressing policy problems unaddressed. Evidence of this increasing polarization can be seen in recent food legislation where partisan support was lopsided. The 2014 Farm Bill was supported by a majority of Republicans and was opposed by a majority of Democrats. However, some Democrats did support the bill, so it is not obvious things are as dire as scholars claim. Furthermore, parties in recent years are not as unified as assumed. Rural "Blue Dog" Democrats would not support the Democrats' Affordable Care Act, while "Tea Party" Republicans have frequently challenged House and Senate Republican leadership. Likewise, Republican congressional leaders searched for common ground with a populist president in Trump.

The Players and Food Policy

When it comes to looking at the players, we are interested in team behavior on food and farm policy. In the rest of the book, we will examine the players at two levels. First, in the next two chapters, we will look at the historic food policy work of the teams and their players (Chapters 4 and 5). Second, in Chapter 6, we will look at team stats, comparing red players to blue players in their support for specific food policies and seeing what each team has been doing. To what extent do members of each team work together? Under what conditions will a player actually move the ball down the field for the *other* team? Is there a red and blue food policy? We will also examine presidential behavior with regard to food policy. Of particular interest is the degree to which red and blue presidents differ on food policy. Furthermore, if we are interested in a red and blue pattern to food policy, we can examine food policy approaches in red and blue states, to see if there is a partisan pattern.

In terms of food policy, we would expect these trends to surface in our study of partisan behavior and food. The purported bi-partisanship of food policy may have been nothing more than Midwestern Republican support for New Deal farm bills or Southern Democratic support for Republican farm bills. This does not necessarily mean that the party itself is pursuing a bipartisan food agenda. This leads us to the second part of the team, the coaches.

The Coaching Staff

Like any team, political parties need a coaching staff—to recruit candidates, coordinate team play, and to mobilize support. This coaching staff is in the party organizations themselves. Known nationally as the Democratic National Committee (DNC) and the Republican National Committee (RNC) these are federated organizations with staff at local and national levels to assist in player recruitment and election. Locally, Republicans and Democrats are organized at the precinct level, U.S. House district level, and state level. These local staffers recruit and assist candidates for local, state and federal offices. The national coaching staff collects party donations and distributes them to candidates across the nation, especially those in vulnerable or important races.

Like any professional or college team organization, the team's staff recruits candidates and mobilizes support. In politics, this means the local precinct or Congressional district team staff will look around for good men and women to wear their jersey in an election. Local precincts may look for community leaders or business owners to approach to run for office. Congressional districts may look at "J.V." teams, like local state assembly members or state senators to recruit to wear their jersey in a congressional race.

Team staff will also work to mobilize fan support for the team. Precincts may field volunteers to go door-to-door to drum up support for the team's candidates. Congressional districts and national organizations may fund expensive telephone banks or mass mailings to reach fans. As a professional sports organization spends money advertising the team, team logo and popular players in television and print media, the political party teams spend to advertise their agenda and their players. Locally they may print and post signs. Nationally they may give money so candidates can produce television commercials and social media campaigns in favor of their candidate and against their opponents.

This staff work has important implications for food and agriculture policy. All politics is local, and local politics may be dominated by major food players, such as Archer Daniels Midland in central Illinois or Bayer in Saint Louis, or any large employer who also deals in food (Hershey Pennsylvania) or farming products (John Deere in Moline, Illinois or Waterloo, Iowa). Local politics in rural areas may also be dominated by farmers, who control assets and usually hold prominent community positions, while in others it may be dominated by foodies, retirees, suburbanites or grass roots millennials who push for a more progressive local food and agriculture agenda. The coaching staff and the players have to be sensitive to powerful, parochial (local) interests.

The national coaching staff also organizes a party convention every four years to formulate official party positions on every conceivable issue. Staff and volunteers from precincts and states attend the convention and provide their input to the official party agenda. The resulting document is published as the official Democrat or Republican Party Platform, listing the team goals for every area of policy, including farm policy or rural policy, as it is commonly called in the published "Party Platform". Of course the same convention, rotating in different "stadiums" each year, also nominates the party's candidate for president.

The Party Playbook

If we want to vote with our fork and support a political party based on its food policy agenda, published party platforms are an excellent way to know where the party stands. It's kind of like a *playbook*, signaling how the team will approach each issue. Reading the playbook is the most direct way to see what the party plans to do or hopes to do. The red and blue teams' playbooks lay out approaches to commodity policy, environmental policy, welfare policy, and so on. It's all there for the foodie and farmer to see, in plain language. In chapter 7 we will compare recent party platforms to see where the more ideologically coherent unified teams are taking American food policy, and just how similar or different their playbook reads.

The Fans

Like any fan, most American voters have an affinity for one political party or the other. Scholars refer to the fans as the Party in the Electorate, the ordinary citizens who identify with a political party. Unlike in other nations, Americans rarely join political parties and become card carrying members in any formal sense, nor do most participate in party organization activities. Instead, they are more like fans—

they root for the red or blue team at a distance, talking about their favorites to their friends at work or in the neighborhood café, and following them in the media.

Like a sports fan, rooting for a political party or a particular player is somewhat of a psychological attachment. A fan will have an almost automatic favorable response to players wearing "their" jersey and an almost unfavorable or skeptical response to a player or team in the other jersey. Red team fans will give red team players the benefit of the doubt, and be skeptical or critical of any player or policy of the blue team. Likewise, blue team fans will give blue team players or policies a chance, while maintaining distant or hostile feelings toward members or policies of the red team. Actual voting tends to be more man-to-man, with red or blue voters sometimes crossing party lines to support an individual, particularly an incumbent House member or Senator, who they feel is doing a decent job. Of course, not all Americans are fans, but most do lean red or blue.

If you want to picture American party politics, picture a stadium. The players are on the field, the coaches are on the sidelines, and the fans are in the stands. In hometown stadiums, you expect the hometown team's fans to show up in greater number. The same is true in politics. Blue areas have more blue fans. Red areas have more red fans. In terms of food policy, this particularly happens when urban areas tend to vote blue and rural areas tend to vote red.

Overtime, you might also expect the fans to dominate when their team dominates. Political scientists have mapped out red and blue dominance overtime. As noted above, the Red team, as the party of Lincoln and the victorious North, dominated after the Civil War 1860-1896. The Blue team, as the party of FDR and the New Deal, dominated 1932-1964. For this reason, most voters of the Great Depression era tend to lean Democrat. Most white voters of the South 1869-1980 tend to lean Democrat. When whole groups of fans switch sides or begin rooting for a new team, political scientists call that a realignment. Republicans dominated politics until the Great Depression, when the other team promised a way out. Democrats commanded a large portion of the Southern conservative vote until they embraced forced civil rights and moral tolerance, something problematic for Southern whites and religious conservatives.

In terms of the groups in the stands, there are a few trends when it comes to food policy. In recent years, farmers have tended to favor the red team in their vote choices. Likewise, blue states and urban areas have been leading the effort to reform farm and food practices, such as California measures to restrict egg factories or New York City's tax on soda to fight obesity. This does not mean all farmers vote red and all Californians or New Yorkers vote blue. Historically, fans tended to follow the local team. Southern farmers would vote blue, because the blue team ran the south. Midwest farmers would vote red, because the red team dominated the Midwest. Likewise urban progressives had to operate within the blue team because many blue teams dominated urban party machines.

When it comes to assessing the party in the electorate—the fans—it is difficult to gauge numbers. Studies show Americans more recently tend to identify around 33% Republican and 23% Democrat, with most voters more comfortable with the Independent label.[5] This implies that the party in the electorate is somewhat weak, with most voters up for grabs during each new election. To an extent, this is true in another sense, as well. Simply measuring voter support for a red or blue candidate may not indicate voter identification with the red or blue team. As noted above, many voters vote for the individual, not the jersey, making fan base an allusive measure. Likewise, many voters may dislike an individual, such as Trump or Obama, but only a portion of that dislike may also transfer to Trump's red team or Obama's blue team.

A Few Other Parts of the Game

Sponsors

Lobbyists and interest groups are somewhat like sponsors who independently support players and team agendas. Most sports teams or players have sponsors, and NASCAR and golf are sports that prominently portray team sponsors with stickers on cars or logos sewn onto golf shirts. In food politics, you will not see a red or blue jersey with logos from the major food policy lobbyists sewed on, but it would be fun. Imagine an "American Farm Bureau" patch or a "National Restaurant Association" logo or a "Dairy Council" iron-on. We cannot see the sponsors behind player's decisions, but we know they are there because that is how the game is played.[6]

More importantly, the players actually *need* sponsors to get the job done. In his poignant in-house study of Congress, John Haskell notes that making policy requires information—a lot of information[7] What kind of information matters to legislators? Usually, they need information about the likely outcomes of a particular policy path. For instance, in our complex society, moving one lever might move everything else. If we subsidize corn, we will raise the price of corn products, such as soft drinks and tortilla chips, and the price of meat, which is fattened with corn. If we drop cotton subsidies, we might put small communities with cotton gins out of business. Also, there might be multiple paths to a particular goal, each with its own costs and benefits. If we want to provide children with a better diet, we might increase family SNAP and WIC benefits or we might tinker with federal school lunch regulations or we might fund more effective nutrition education in elementary schools. How is an elected official, like a Congressman, even a Committee chair, to gather the information and research necessary to design an effective policy? According to Haskell, they can't. That is where lobbyists play a useful role, providing legislators with information about approaches to policy problems and effects of policy options. The robust information environment provided by adversarial-minded competing lobbies means that almost no stone is unturned—and our system usually has a good idea how and if a particular policy will work, what it will do, and where it will fall short. Again, the teams and players may disagree on the goals, but they will have fairly good information on the policy options themselves, largely due to the work of sponsors.

In food policy, lobby groups will provide information about how a particular regulation or idea will affect their constituents or about the need for a particular policy. In 2014 organic and grass fed beef producers asked Congress and the USDA for additional guidelines to protect their industries. In 2015, Genetically modified seed producers, farmers, and food manufacturers asked for a uniform federal law regulating GMO labeling to supplant various state-level GMO labeling laws. In 2016, farmer groups began telling Congress to reform the commodity payment program based on county averages, based on data about how that formula actually worked in 2015. This kind of information, albeit somewhat agenda-driven, is useful for policy change and development.

Tournaments

Before we look at historic red and blue wins, losses and plays in food politics, we need to understand the game calendar a little bit. Democrats and Republicans are first of all playing for re-election, and elections represent the key tournaments in players' minds. Every four years, the nation elects a president. This draws more fans to the game, and about 60% of Americans vote in presidential elections. This is the big tournament for players in Congress as well, because everyone is watching and most people are voting! And they are voting for president, House *and* one-third of the Senate. This makes Presidential election years the biggest tournament for political parties. These are even bigger if there is no incumbent candidate, and in recent decades the biggest tournaments are every eight years. As we shall see, a surprising amount of presidential election politics historically centered on food and farm politics.

In between presidential elections are midterm elections. In these elections the red and blue teams are on the ballot in the form of congressional candidates, but their star player, the president is also somewhat competing. Fans show up at the rate of 40%, usually favoring the team that is not in the White house. For this reason it is customary for the president's team to lose seats. This happened to President Bush and Republicans in 2006, when Democrats took over Congress. This also happened to President Obama in 2010, when Republicans took over Congress, and Obama famously quipped that he had been "shellacked."

One other set of elections is also important in team play. Primary elections are typically held earlier in the year to choose the candidates for each team. In recent years, these contests have been quite a free-for-all, with 10 or more players competing for the party nomination in presidential primaries! Primaries are typically dominated by party activists, rabid fans who *really* care about the future of the team. As a result, primary voters often favor more extreme or outlier candidates. This tendency only exacerbates the problem of teams being *poles* apart when they try to govern the nation together. The Primary Game used to be left to the private back-room politics of the coaches and players—the party committees would hold fairly in-house meetings or conventions to nominate candidates. Since the late 1960s, the primary game has been open to fan voting, sponsorship, and populist uprisings—making the whole process more unwieldy. Democratic and Republican Party organizations (coaches) would never have recruited Bernie Sanders or Donald Trump to play for them as president. But the *fans* who attended the primaries did. This is one reason presidents and presidential candidates may seem out-of-touch with the rest of the team and the rest of the fan base in recent years.

Cinderella Teams

Sometimes a third party will challenge the dominant to parties. These can be thought of as Cinderella teams, minority parties that challenged the number one seeds now and again. The Populist Party, a coalition of farmers, did just that to the in the early 1890's winning many local government posts in the upper Midwest. By 1896, the Democratic Party wisely adopted many populist positions in their playbook, effectively absorbing the Populist Party as a branch of their own. More recently Republicans have tried to contain the libertarian leaning "Tea Party" and Democrats have tried to contain the Bernie Sanders-supporting Socialists to keep a more even hand on power.

Team Reputations

One final consideration of team politics is the notion of team reputations. Scholars in political science have recognized that political parties tend to experience "issue ownership"—where they are perceived as more competent to deal with a particular political issue.[8] Recent scholarship has invented the concept of issue ownership to describe what we are discussing in this book—who *owns* the issue of food and farming policy? According to the concept of issue ownership a particular team will get the reputation of being better at certain pressing policy matters. In recent years, the Democratic Party has obtained issue ownership over welfare policy, the environment and civil rights. The Republican Party has obtained issue ownership over national security policy and "law and order". In terms of food policy, one scholar claims the Democrats also own farm policy since 1950,[9] and I have mused elsewhere that this might be the case.[10] That is why I am writing this book—to find out.

Where's the Party?

I hope this discussion has caught you up on the game as it is currently understood and played. Understanding team politics will allow us to view the game of food politics like an expert. We can now examine red and blue strategies and we know what to watch for. Presidential and midterm elections will offer interesting incentives to policy makers and candidates formulating food policy. Congressional leaders will be more partisan and ideological than rank-in-file leaders. Presidents, too, will have their agendas, sometimes at odds with their own team as a result of the primary process. USDA secretaries or other cabinet members might become significant game changers. Sponsors of one agenda or another will tend to favor one team over the other, and fans will have to sort this all out, including farmers and foodies.

---

[1] Smith, Robert C., and Richard A. Seltzer. 2015. *Polarization and the Presidency: From FDR to Barak Obama.* Boulder, CO: Lynne Rienner Publishers.

[2] Fiorina, Morris P. 1980. "The Decline of Collective Responsibility in American Politics," *Daedalus* 71: 883-917.

[3] Neustadt, Richard. 1960. *Presidential Power.* New York: John Wiley & Sons, Inc.

[4] Rae, Nicol. 2007. "Be Careful what you wish for: The Rise of Responsible Parties in American National Politics." Annual Review of Political Science. vol. 10.

[5] Pew Research Center. 2015. "A Deep Dive into Party Affiliation" April 7, 2015 http://www.people-press.org/2015/04/07/a-deep-dive-into-party-affiliation/ last accessed March 17, 2017.

[6] For an exhaustive treatment of the players and sponsors in the food industry, Marion Nestle's *Food Politics: How the Food Industry Influences Nutrition and Health* (University of California Press, 2013) is an excellent source.

[7] Haskell, John. 2010. *Congress in Context.* Boulder CO: Westview Press.

[8] Petrocik, J.R. 1996. "Issue Ownership in Presidential Elections, with a 1980 Case Study." *American Journal of Political Science* 40:825-850.; Petrocik, John R., William L. Benoit, Glenn J. Hansen. 2003. "Issue Ownership and Presidential Campaigning, 1952-2000." *Political Science Quarterly* 188:599-626.

[9] Petrocik, John R., William L. Benoit, Glenn J. Hansen. 2003. "Issue Ownership and Presidential Campaigning, 1952-2000." *Political Science Quarterly* 188:599-626.

[10] Harris, Rebecca C. 2016. The Political Identity of Food: Partisan Implications of the New Food Politics." *Food Studies: An Interdisciplinary Journal* 6(4):1-20.

Chapter 3

Before Welfare: Lessons from Early Farm Politics

We need to set the stage in farm politics *before* welfare—to understand how farmers whose ancestors single-handedly settled a wilderness could suddenly demand government help. The answer is that, like most things in history, it is not sudden at all. In fact, farmer demands for financial help started before the U.S. Constitution was written, before there were Democratic and Republican parties.

The Agrarian Ideal

Farms and farmers have a very special place in historical American culture. Ask most Americans what they think of farmers and the image is typically a good one. Farmers get up early, work hard, raise good families, and contribute to society. Farmers also enjoy a high level of trust compared to other actors in the food industry.[1] This good will can translate into political sympathy, making farms and farmers worthy of political support. The imagery of farming has always had a virtuous side. Since the time of the Founders, farming symbolized independent, peaceful, and productive life. Settlers in the wilderness and "frontiers" of the East Coast (New England, Western Pennsylvania, Western Virginia, Western Carolinas, etc.) sustained themselves by farming the land. Later pioneers carved out productive lives from harsh prairies and rangelands. The images of the barn, the wagon or the cowboy hat are iconic American symbols of determination, grit, hard work and promise, words and American values that still find a place in American electoral values today.

Thomas Jefferson famously lauded these Americans in his writings, and he expected farmers and farm life to underpin the young democracy. In his *Notes on the State of Virginia*, he called for a nation of "husbandmen...free and beholden to no one."[2] To Jefferson, farmers were virtuous and moral in comparison to the manufacturing and commerce classes—where greed, exploitation of labor, and the necessary dependence and subservience of the worker were the norm. Farming, itself, because of private property ownership, was viewed by Jefferson as a source of economic security. Hence, the beauty of Jefferson's Louisiana Purchase was the eventual availability of land for any willing worker to "prove up" and claim an independent living under later homesteading laws. The pioneers who settled the Ohio Valley, the Upper Midwest and the American West did just this with their frontier farms and ranches. America was known as a nation of independent farmers—hardy families farming land they owned or claimed.

The Political Reality

National policies toward farming, however, have historically been about money and very material concerns: debt, private property, and economics, particularly farm incomes and food prices. To understand American farm politics is to understand the tension between the romantic agrarian ideal of virtuous productive pastoral living and to understand that, ultimately, politics is about money and self-interest.

The history of early farm politics essentially follows the old political adage to *follow the money*. Here the money is to be found in middlemen (railroads, packers, processors) and in bankers—not necessarily the farmers themselves. Even today, modern farmers receive about 17% of every food dollar.[3] Part of the history of farm politics is an attempt to tip the balance of money back to the producers. The other part is to keep that credit flowing—and if bankers will not loan money, the federal government will.

American farm politics is not necessarily virtuous or pastoral when it came to actual politics, and early farm political stories are characterized by unrest and unhappiness. As noted in Chapter One, farmers are usually debtors who have to borrow capital for the inputs of their enterprise: land, seed, labor and other expenses. At harvest, they sell the crop and pay their debts. This means they are at the mercy of the creditors (and their interest rates), the wholesaler, the shipper, and the weather. If a farmer had a poor year, a creditor could seize his land for payment—leaving him destitute, with no way to make a living. This relationship naturally sets up a tension between those with the capital and those who need it. In other words, policies which benefit creditors would naturally encumber debtors.

Revolutionary Farmers

At the time of the Founding, farmers actually turned to violence in their war with creditors. Between the American Revolution (1776) and the forming of the United

States via the U.S. Constitution (1789), each of the thirteen colonies was a sovereign state with its own form of government and its own legislative practices. One of these roles was the printing of paper money, and in the times following the revolution, paper money was in short supply. To print more money would have effect (as it does in modern times) of devaluing debts because they become easier to pay back. While some states printed more currency to assist debtors, other states, such as Massachusetts did not. The resulting politics pitted Eastern Massachusetts merchant creditors against Western Massachusetts farmers who were losing their land.

The conflict came to a head in a 4000-man rebellion led by Daniel Shay right before the Constitutional Convention in 1787, a rebellion put down by militias financed largely by Boston merchants. The Framers of the Constitution took note, and the unrest led to several provisions and discussions of debt and the printing of currency (among other issues) for those envisioning the role of a new Federal government. Ultimately the new Constitution gave the newly formed U.S. Congress the power to print money and to absorb the state debts incurred by the Revolutionary war, alleviating pressure on all sides.

Politics has been consistently responsive to farmers. The conflict between bankers, merchants and farmers highlights a reoccurring theme throughout American history, and even modern farm policy is heavily focused on helping the debtor farmer. Demand for political responsiveness to farm needs was always a factor for elected representatives because American voters were overwhelmingly farm and rural-based for much of U.S. history prior to 1900. During this time farmers enjoyed significant political strength, especially at the local and state level. America was a nation of mostly small freeholders, and most families had ties "back to the farm" until the second wave of immigration at the turn of the century, lending a majoritarian appeal to farmers' pleas. Local officeholders had to be kind to farmers to remain in office, regardless of party.

Farmers, Welfare and the Coming New Deal

All of this changed in the 20th Century. The history of modern farm policy is essentially a history of a social welfare program, and that means Democrats and Republicans will typically feel differently about helping the poor farmer with federal dollars. Like most social programs, the crux of the story starts with the New Deal and perhaps a little before. Farmers, like everyone else, were hurting and there was a political incentive to do something about it.

Farmers, as a class, are not your typical welfare recipients. When our story begins (c. 1900), farmers and farm families were roughly 30-40% of the population and control significant assets, particularly in a local sense. The average farm size in 1900 was 138 acres. (Today less than 2% of Americans are farmers, and the average farm is about 434 acres.)[4] Furthermore, good economic times in the early 20th Century placed farmers in a strong community and economic position. Even more important for majoritarian politics, farmers were viewed as hardworking, independent citizens—with many voters historically connected to farm life. Farmers were also politically active, especially locally, and usually leveraged additional community ties through religious and community organizations. Until the New Deal, most agricultural concerns were regulated at the state level. Thus early farm politics has been termed "provincial" by most scholars—largely local in scope.

In terms of national politics in 1900, the concerns of farmers coincided with the concerns of urban progressives of the time, building momentum for more national cooperation on policy. Farmers were concerned with banks, railroads, and processors who monopolized their opportunities to bring crops to market. Progressives in the big cities were concerned with industrialization's impact on the ordinary working family and on American life more generally. Together, the voting force of farmers and the progressive appeal of their principle concerns set up a significant political demand for services. Parties could not ignore this demand.

Both parties were somewhat farm-based in 1900. Since the Civil War, the Republican Party was dominant in American politics—and its dominance meant that it could not ignore farm demands and stay in power, especially since rural districts tend hold disproportionate voting power. On the other hand, by 1900 the Democratic Party had absorbed many populist and progressive demands in both their rural and urban strongholds, in effect aligning them with farmer's material demands. As the rest of the book argues, this political situation has changed drastically, with neither party's modern agenda particularly receptive to a modern farmer's material concerns. Modern Republicans tend to be skeptical of government subsidies for farmers and farm programs. Modern Democrats tend to support additional farm production regulation, raising the cost of doing business. For now, we will explore the early partisan history of Farm policy 1896—1932, to understand the partisan beginnings of farm welfare policy.

The Last Farmer's Party

America came the closest to a Farmer's party during the election of 1896. The Populist Party of the 1890's was, in part, a grassroots action program developed by farmers in the South, West and Midwest suffering from economic downturns. With all the surprise of "Cinderella Team," the Populist Party won many seats at the state level in the 1890's, including governorships. The Populist movement sought to use democracy (majority rules) to rein in the financial gains of business, industry and commerce, and enjoyed quite a bit of success at the state level. In 1896, following on now age-old concerns about credit, this third party had called for the free coinage of silver and a vastly expanded supply of paper money—inflationary measures which would benefit farmers as debtors. They also called for government ownership of the railroads and the elimination of monopolies. These appeals were very popular with farmer voters.

As one might imagine, the dominant political parties did not appreciate a Cinderella team stealing victories at the state level and threatening to win the presidency. Trying to gain vote share, the 1896 Democratic Party Platform adopted many of the concerns of the populists—but also defeating the Populist candidate and signaling the collapse of the effort to build a farmers party. The victorious Democratic Party made good on some of these co-opted issues and the populist movement contributed to federal regulation of railroads and the passage of the Sherman Anti-Trust Act. Dovetailing with the agrarian populists was the urban progressive movement, that also found a home in the Democratic party, seeking to use government to address the economic and social problems of rapid industrialization, further cementing the social welfare tendencies of the blue team.

As party competitions often go, the red team did not stand on sidelines. To regain office, Republicans *also* had to adopt some of these populist demands. Under Republican President Teddy Roosevelt in 1901, the federal government expanded its attacks on monopolies ("trust busting") and increased federal regulation of business. Progressives also pushed for majority democratic tools, such as initiatives and referendums, to provide more majority control over state-level commerce policy. In general, there was the recognition among progressives *and* farmers that politics could be a counterweight to industry power and the monopolies of railroads, grain merchants, processors and banks. (A similar sentiment is afoot in many progressive food movements today seeking ways to undo monopolies in food production supported by government support.)

One other development set the stage for farm development policy, particularly on the Republican side. Progressive reforms of Congress, itself, weakened party ability to control their members. In the House, the power of the Speaker and the patronage system was curtailed in favor of stronger committee power. This set the stage for farm groups to penetrate specialist committees, even when parties were unresponsive.[5] With the backing of farm groups and their votes back home, individual officeholders from farm regions had the political power to defy their *own* party leadership to support farmers.

Roaring Twenties, Warring Republicans

Just this scenario led to the first major federal farm policies.[6] In 1921, sympathetic Republican Senators passed progressive-style reforms demanded by farmers *against* larger party leadership, which supported a more *laissez-faire* approach to the economy. Passed with support from Democrats, these reforms regulated meatpackers, milk distributors, and grain exchanges as well as extended a World War I farm loan program. This move by the early Farm Bloc foreshadowed and even bigger Republican war to come between Congress and the president. When

Congress sought to directly intervene into the farm economy in 1927, the Republican president, Calvin Coolidge, felt that his fellow Congressmen were playing for the other team.

To understand the story of these "warring Republicans", one has to understand the economic setting of the times. During World War I, Europe had to import a great deal of American agricultural products due to the war's disruption of their food production. This led to record high prices for American farm products, and a generation of American farmers realized true prosperity for the first time. For this generation of farmers, 1919 is the magic year when farm prices were high and times on the farm were really good. The year would be referenced for decades to come in the concept of "parity", a bench mark for when prices for crops were higher than costs to produce the crop. After the war, prices plummeted as Europe recovered and new producers elsewhere in the world, particularly Argentina, Australia and Russia entered the scene. Compared to the rest of America, U.S. farmers watched from the sidelines of the Roaring Twenties—everyone seemed to be making money but farmers.

Yet, 70% of Americans still lived in rural areas at this time, and this meant the farmer's plight had the attention of both teams in Congress. In response Republicans crafted in 1927 the first farm subsidy bill. However, their own President, Calvin Coolidge, refused to sign it! Here is where we see the first modern party activity on behalf of farmers—and it arose from the team in power, the Republicans.

The problem, as the politicians defined it, was that farmers were not getting enough money for their crops to cover costs, let alone have something left to live on. (This problem is somewhat timeless and surprisingly contemporary, with many 2018 farmers also experiencing prices below the cost of production and a large portion of contemporary American farms survive with off-farm income from outside jobs.) The solution in 1927 was to find a way to raise prices so farm economy could be sustainable. The plan was for the federal government to buy surplus farm products, thereby raising their price for the farmer (And for everyone else!). The government would then sell the products on the export market at a loss, a practice commonly criticized in today's world as "dumping." The *1927 McNary-Haugen Bill* was drafted by two Republicans from Oregon and Iowa, to assist grain farmers.

However, to gain enough Congressional support the bill also included cotton and tobacco programs to appease Southern Democrats, providing the first hint of the canon of bi-partisanship in farm policy. *McNary-Haugen* is the policy which gave birth to the storied bipartisan Farm Bloc in Congress. Bi-partisanship was based on *material* concerns with geographically rooted economic concerns creating cross-partisan pressures. The Republican Midwest and Northwest members of Congress had districts and states full of corn and wheat farmers. Southern Democratic members of Congress in the South had districts and states full of tobacco and cotton growers. While the parties did not normally cooperate, rural representatives found that their constituents had quite a lot in common when it came to farm business.

Republican President Coolidge wanted no part of it, and here is where the Republican war started. Unlike *local*, materially-minded representatives from these farming regions, *national* party leaders, such as Coolidge, were somewhat less material and more ideological and *partisan* in their federal policy approach. Republicans then (as now) wanted less federal government involvement in economic matters. President Coolidge's veto speech of the *McNary-Haugen Bill* echoes these principles, providing insight into the foundation of true red team approaches to welfare for farmers. In rejecting the 1927 bill, Coolidge stated:

> This mistake leads away from a permanent solution. It is a fundamental economic problem that cannot be solved by political action. Federal action on behalf of agriculture [should] assist in the organization to build up marketing agencies and facilities in the control of farmers themselves. I want to see them undertake, under their own management, the marketing of their products under such conditions as will enable them to bring about greater stability in prices and less waste in marketing, but entirely within unalterable economic laws. Such a program is in accordance with the American tradition and the American ideal of reliance on and maintenance of private initiative and individual responsibility.[7]

The speech is quite contemporary in its conservative language. The Republican Party of today makes the *same* appeal to private initiative and individual responsibility when asked to intervene on behalf of the welfare of Americans. More technically, the speech is somewhat prophetic in its anticipation of the cooperative farm movement and modern governmental mechanisms enabling the organization of private marketing firms for American farm products. Republicans and conservatives tend to value private, cooperative assistance as less intrusive into free-market economics than direct government intervention. Today, farmers work together through government chartered monopolies called "co-operatives", such as the Dairy Farmers of America, which pool resources and buying power for farm inputs and for marketing and sales contracts—allowing them to employ economies of scale and professional expertise when competing with the industrial corporations which supply their inputs and purchase their products. Farmers also enjoy the fruit of corn and soybean and beef and other "check-offs" where a portion of every bushel or animal sold is put in the coffers of a government chartered private marketing firm, such as Cotton Incorporated, which works to open new markets and products for American products—just as President Coolidge suggested. The 2018 Farm Bill has even considered chartering an Organic Grower check-off for organic farmers.

This brief quote also highlights the essential feeling of Republican conservative ideology toward federal welfare programs. Coolidge understood the "fundamental economic problem" and the "unalterable laws of economics" such as supply and demand. In the farm sector, welfare for farmers meant higher consumer prices and created an incentive for farmers to overproduce—which had the effect of lowering prices again, further exacerbating the problem with each new season. Coolidge understood that if the government tinkered with markets to make farming artificially profitable, it would attract more farm production, not less, which because of increased supply, will lower prices even further. That meant that because of *McNary-Haugen*, future circumstances would require *additional* government spending to prop it up, making the entire program fiscally and economically unsustainable. Moreover, artificial prices would also decrease efficiency, allowing those operations which are not profitable to stay in business longer. These are the economic principles which make free-market policies so reasonable to Republicans. With Coolidge's speech it is easy to anticipate the way ideological Republican free market advocates will seek to dismantle farm programs when they next gain significant control of Congress in 1995.

Parochial Politics

One might also wonder why independent minded farmers suddenly wanted government help. The answer is because things were *so* bad. Most of us will sell our ideological soul when our very security is on the line. The answer, too, lies in the fact that it was not really sudden at all: earlier generations had demanded government's help in the downturn of the 1890s and gave rise to the Populist Party. It is also prophetic that the key is *parochial* (local) political demands. It was local Midwest and Southern farm demands not the party that drove Congressional goals.

This has important implications for food policy today. If food policy is essentially local policy, and if the local politics demands change, politicians of either stripe will bend to the clamor. This also means that if the foodies overtake the farmers in local political power, food policy will favor the foodies. This has real implications for the Democratic Party—a historical supporter of traditional farm price supports. Furthermore, if the local foodies favor specialty crops (fruits and vegetables) instead of commodities (grains and fibers) or if they favor grass-fed beef over feed-lot beef or organic crops over conventional crops, food policy will begin to favor what the local foodies are telling their Congressional representatives they want. Furthermore, policies will change even more quickly at the local level—especially in cities. This is why we will examine food policy at the state level, taking a cue from the Populist success of the 19th century.

Lessons for Farm Politics

As this chapter has demonstrated, traditional farm policy, like most everything else, is about money—and policies about money traditionally divide modern day political parties. One party wants to use money to address social welfare concerns. The other party feels that wealth is generated by a properly functioning market with minimal government tinkering. This implies that Democrats will gravitate toward farm support policies and that Republicans will be skeptical of government intervention into the farm economy.

On the other hand, Democrats and Republicans are elected by local constituencies with local needs. To stay in office, representatives have to represent *local* concerns. With many districts rural and farm-based, these needs naturally revolved around the state of the farm economy. Furthermore, with the rise of progressivism, it became popular to demand government intervention into the free-for-all economics of the industrial revolution, giving farmers a political place to turn in the face of daunting economic prospects. And they turned to their representatives in Congress. These early experiences with seeking government support created the demand for farm programs which finally came of age in the New Deal.

---

[1] Marcus Glassman. 2015. Hungry for Information: Polling Americans on Their Trust in the Food System. Chicago Council on Global Affiars. October 2015.
https://www.thechicagocouncil.org/publication/hungry-information-polling-americans-their-trust-food-system Last accessed May 2, 2017.

[2] Jefferson, Thomas. 1964. *Notes on the State of Virginia* (New York, NY: Harper and Row Publishers, 1964).

[3] National Farmers Union. 2016. The Farmer's Share. https://nfu.org/farmers-share/ Last Accessed May 2, 2017.

[4] USDA. 2014. 2012 Census Highlights. May 2014
https://www.agcensus.usda.gov/Publications/2012/Online_Resources/Highlights/Farm_Demographics/ Last Accessed May 2, 2017.

[5] Hansen, John Mark. 1991. *Gaining Access: Congress and the Farm Lobby*. Chicago: University of Chicago Press.

[6] Much of this section is borrowed from John Mark Hansen's excellent history of early farm policy.

[7] 1928 Calvin Coolidge Veto Speech

Chapter 4

Heroes, Villains & Legacies of New Deal Progressivism

Food policy has traditionally been about *farmers*—not necessarily food or those who eat food—at least not at first. This is important to grasp, as it sets up the political story. Telling a history story can get pretty boring, pretty fast if we don't understand the plot, and our story has to introduce us to the "heroes and villains" of bipartisan food policy. Thus, the bipartisan history of food & farming is really a story about Presidents, members of Congress (especially chairs of the House and Senate Agriculture Committees), and secretaries of the USDA. In this context, heroes are those who are fighting "for the farmer", especially those who are willing to work with members of the other team in a bipartisan manner. The heroes usually fight for the farmer to win the farmer's vote, and much of the story is truly a story of two teams competing for farm votes. Heroes may also be committed to the actual policy of helping farmers and other beneficiaries of farm policy.

Villains are those who are working on something else, usually making them the enemy of the farmer[1] Villains are those who do not have to worry about the farm vote, either because they have other political supporters or because they are not in elected office, such as a USDA secretary. Villains are also those who disagree with the farmers' political agenda or other parts of farm policy (especially if it involves federal dollars or federal control of the economy) or those who want to help someone else—like the consumer or tax payer. Heroes and villains wear team jerseys, too, and play for political teams to win political goals. Food policy is a story of two teams competing to win elections and to implement policy goals. Other experts try to paint the story as one of cooperation[2], but that is just not the case. The Red team and the Blue team have different goals and different fans, and they are just not going to see the world the same way. Since this story is not a novel, I am going to go ahead and name names, so you can keep track of the characters. But first, a caveat: By using such loaded terms as hero and villain, I have opened myself to instant criticism if a reader happens to be one of those citizens rooting against the conventional farm policy agenda. Even conventional farmers do not necessarily support these policies, and conservatives, environmentalists and those concerned with public health may also question the policy—or even root for the villains! However, this story is being told from the perspective of those who support conventional farm policy to make it easy to tell who is doing what.

So, back to naming names: The heroes of the story (from the perspective of supporting conventional farm policy) are first, and foremost, the congressional Farm Bloc, committee members of both teams who are more committed to farm politics than party politics. Also in the Heroes column is President Franklin Delano Roosevelt and his Secretary of Agriculture, Henry A. Wallace, as well as the New Deal with its federal support for the farm economy. The villains of the story are mostly Presidents. On the Democratic Team, Harry Truman and John Kennedy alienated the farm vote with intrusive farm policy plans that threatened to tell the farmer when and what to plant. Lukewarm supporters such as Bill Clinton, Barak Obama and Lyndon Johnson paid lip service to farmers but did not fight for stronger farm programs, though they did support the more liberal parts of contemporary farm bills, such as nutrition and conservation. Farm policy itself just isn't high on the modern Democratic presidential agenda. Republican Presidents, however, have always had strong feelings about farm programs and these generally placed them in the villain's column. President Calvin Coolidge, Dwight Eisenhower, Richard Nixon, Ronald Reagan, George W. Bush and Donald Trump, not to mention 1964 presidential candidate, Barry Goldwater, were hostile to or skeptical of farm programs, giving speeches, presenting budgets drastically reducing farm programs or vetoing farm bills altogether. Also on the villain side are Republicans in Congress who are not committed to farm programs, especially House Speaker Newt Gingrich and his Congressional allies in 1996 which changed farm support programs forever. During the deliberations over the 2014 and 2018 farm bills, Republican "Freedom Caucus" members also worked tirelessly to dismantle farm programs. More importantly, the most vilified names in farm policy are actually USDA secretaries Charles Brannan (Truman), Ezra Taft Benson (Eisenhower), Orville Freeman (Kennedy), and, notably, Earl Butz (Nixon), who had the public servant's audacity to suggest changing food policy to benefit federal coffers and consumers more than farmers.

In general, as the story reveals, farm program support is more at home with Democrats than Republicans, with Congress more than presidents, and with the Farm Bloc more than the rest of Congress. The story also reveals that USDA secretaries do not necessarily support traditional farm programs—and much of the agency is more progressive or more conservative—seeking to serve someone other than the farmer.

Setting the Stage: Farmers on Welfare in a Capitalist Society

The main problem in our story is that farm policy is really about giving farmers federal dollars to stay in business—and this idea tends to divide the red team from the blue team. The history of modern farm policy in the United States is essentially the history of a social welfare policy—a policy designed to prop up the incomes of farm families. Most nations, especially in Europe, see farmers and farm policy as a social welfare policy, typically subsidizing the business of farming as a national policy to promote domestic food supply and the farm economy. As a nation of independent, hardworking, self-sufficient citizens and immigrants, America has always been more likely to embrace capitalism and less likely to expect government support than nations with a history of kings, vassals and peasants.[3] This means America is much more centrist and market-oriented in its economic policy, making welfare the exception rather than rule.

But what is a "social welfare policy" anyway? In short, it is a policy where government gets involved and expends resources to help someone out. But it is not always as obviously good as it sounds. Government gets "involved" by throwing its weight around—expanding its authority. In this context, government expanded its authority into the food and farm economy Big Time. Political scientist, Adam Shiengate, characterized American agriculture as a welfare state policy based on the way it operated.[4] As Sheingate notes, American farm policies originated with the expanding government authority of the New Deal. The Agricultural Adjustment Acts of 1933 gave the federal government new power to intervene in the agricultural economy--setting prices and controlling farm production decisions by literally telling a farmer what to plant and what price he could receive. Social welfare policies also resemble social insurance—meaning they redistribute resources—in this case from taxpayers to farmers. Commodity programs, by allowing farmers to sell their products at a government-specified price (or more technically borrow and repay with crops at a specified price), resembled "sector specific social insurance" according to Sheingate. Also, as we might expect social welfare policy tends to operate as a safety net—it is designed to provide a minimum income to families—in this case, farm families. The purpose of the program was to help farm families' household income, an approach similar to Social Security or Aid to Families with Dependent Children—two major New Deal-era social welfare policies. The expansion of government authority into the farm economy, the insured prices of government programs and the goal of providing a safety net for families make farm policy a social welfare policy.

Social welfare also has a political downside, and farm policy no different. Social welfare policy is subject to criticism in discussions of fiscal discipline (budget cuts) and excessive government intervention into the economy, partly because of America's openness to capitalism.[5] These are certainly the touch points with historic and modern critics of farm policy.[6] Historic and modern free market advocates criticize federal attempts to artificially prop up the farm market.

By definition a free market is one allowed to operate with the invisible hand of supply, demand and price. Economists explain the free market approach this way: "if the government just leaves the market alone, it will adjust and result in the most efficient economy."[7] The virtue of this approach is an efficient allocation of resources. Sure, some farmers may go out of business, but that is okay. The overall production of food will use less resources and the farmer can go to work where he (or she) is needed in the labor market. As noted in the last chapter, President Coolidge called intervention in the farm economy contrary to the "unalterable laws of economics."

Also of concern is the fact that taxpayers have to pay for farm support programs, diverting resources from other uses. Many of the "villains" in the story of farm support subscribe to these values and recent farm politics demonstrate continued commitments to dismantle farm programs. In 2014, Freedom Caucus Republicans in the House refused to vote for the farm bill on free-market and budgetary principles, even going so far as to divorce the nutrition title from the farm bill itself in an effort to derail *Democratic* support for farm programs.[8] In 2017, the conservative Heritage Foundation put out policy papers to Congress criticizing wasteful farm programs, in hopes of influencing the development of the 2018 Republican farm bill.[9] Republican President Trump's budget asked Congress to slash USDA spending by 21%.[10]

Since social welfare policy is typically the purview of the Democratic Party, one might wonder how it is that experts in agricultural policy continually refer to it as bi-partisan or even non-partisan. This suggests the Republican Party has played a somewhat even and central role in supporting farm policy as well. How can this be? And why? The purpose of this chapter is to introduce the reader to the partisan history of farm policy in an attempt to unravel the puzzle of bi-partisan support for this particular social welfare policy.

Setting the Stage: Team Politics, Principles and Parochialism

A second main problem in our story is that two themes compete for attention among our heroes and villains: party principles and parochialism (localism). On the one hand, red and blue approaches to food policy are really about red and blue approaches to social welfare programs and the free market economy. These are the *principles* that guide Republicans and Democrats in their thinking. On the other hand, red and blue approaches to food policy need to win elections at the end of the day. Since elections are local and geographically-based, this brings quite a bit of *parochialism* (local preferences) into the mix. One might expect that principles and parochialism would align—after all why would a district elect red or blue leaders if they did not agree with red or blue principles? The answer is that sometimes those voters are looking at other principles than the ones which have to do with social welfare or free-market economics in *food* policy. In fact, it may be the opposite: farmers may be frustrated with handouts for others, but feel they are absolutely necessary for themselves. Foodies may generally support federal intervention in the economy for labor or safety reasons, but eschew government regulations for small farmers or raw milk or hemp production. Thus, farmers may elect a red representative to hold the line on expanding welfare for others and inadvertently elect someone who is not particularly fond of farm welfare either. Foodies may elect a blue representative to ensure federal health and safety regulation for most industries, not realizing that same heavy-handed regulatory approach is going to make everything a progressive farmer, like Joel Salatin of Polyface Farms, wants to do "illegal."[11] As we will see, partisan fights are often the result of parochial economic (material) needs conflicting with partisan principles, which are more ideological.

Another part of the problem is that Congress and presidents simply operate in different institutional environments. Literally, the game looks different and feels different from their vantage point. Presidents, their administrations and their party leaders in Congress are often broadly focused on developing a satisfying and winning partisan agenda. They are dedicated to the entire fan base, especially those activists with season tickets who attend every game. Satisfaction, in part, arises from adherence to *ideological goals,* which many presidents and party leaders keep front and center. For Republicans, these are documented as typically free-market in nature. For Democrats, these are typically New Deal interventionist in nature. Recent scholarship confirms these approaches as a key dividing point in partisan approaches.[12] Therefore, presidents and party leaders in Congress will seek to pursue policies consistent with ideological goals.

By contrast, rank-in-file House representatives and Senators must win local elections to stay in office. This makes them attentive to much more *parochial or material* goals for their districts and states. It is like they are playing the game for their section of fans in the stands, and sometimes those fans may want them to run the ball the other way. In this spirit, regardless of party, Congressmen from rural districts and farm states will typically pursue farm support policies. Furthermore, farm support needs will vary according to geography because different crops are grown in different parts of the country: wheat in Kansas, corn in Iowa, cotton in the South, dairy in the Great Lakes and Northeast, even apples in Washington State. Therefore, regardless of party, members of Congress have some incentive to support policies that support parochial farm products.

Furthermore, as an income support policy for farmers (and more recently SNAP recipients), food policy is inherently subject to ideological disagreements. As noted above, income support for farmers is essentially a federal social welfare policy. It is also a market intervention. Both of these characteristics presuppose that New Deal Democrats and Free-market Republicans will disagree about this policy, with Democrats predisposed to support and Republicans predisposed to non-support. Furthermore, the Farm Bill, itself, also contains other "interventions" that are equally potentially polarizing—especially anti-poverty programs (in the form of SNAP benefits) and regulatory compliance. As anti-poverty programs expand and environmental programs move from voluntary to regulatory, ideological differences become harder to reconcile. Conservatives may balk at a food-stamp or regulation-laden farm bill. Liberals may be concerned about subsidies for "wealthy" farmers and agribusiness. More recent fights about Western land use and farm animal rights simply exacerbate the debate about the proper role of government in agricultural production and the food provision market. How have parties negotiated these institutional and ideological challenges? And what has this done for partisanship or bipartisanship in farm policy?

As alluded to in the last chapter, we expect government leaders to always keep *both* in front of them—they want to follow their principles but they have to win elections. It was much easier for Democrats to follow their principles and win elections when they were *rural*. Once they became urban, they needed new local material reasons for supporting farm and food policy at the expense of federal spending for other, more urbanely helpful programs such as infrastructure, crime control, or additional poverty assistance. It was much harder for Republicans to follow their principles on farm programs and win rural elections until the resurgence of anti-federal sentiment in the 1980s in the form of state's rights opposed to federal regulation of Western range land and any number of environmental laws. Once the farmers and other rural citizens became more concerned with keeping government off their backs and out of their business, Republicans had something ideologically to offer the rural voter.

Tell me 'bout the Good ole Days

Storytellers do not work in a vacuum. Their stories arise from stories they have heard or read about elsewhere. Two previous storytellers figure prominently into the story of modern farm politics: political scientists John Mark Hansen and Adam Sheingate. These scholars examined farm policy to document lobbyist and farm policy development. Along the way, their research also documented partisan behavior toward farm policy, as a kind of side-effect, even though they were not focused on parties. By reanalyzing their work for the partisan story, I am able to use their close analysis of congressional proceedings as a reliable secondary source for information on political parties and farm policy. Thus, the following story is partly a retelling of their facts for *my* story line—a story about how political parties have approached food and farm policy, and I will mention them and their observations often. While their stories were about something else, they offer a lot of facts and insight into our tale of two parties, and I directly reference them when I use their notes on the politics of the times. Of course, most of the work is my own additional research into the partisan story of farm policy.

Our story starts with the "Good old Days." This was back when horse power was still *horse* power on many farms, no electricity, almost no tractors. But in 1917-1919, times were good for American farmers. Grain prices were riding high on Europe's war time farmland disruption. Farmers were catching up on modern amenities, and they felt prosperous because they were prosperous. They were able to sell their grain and other food products for much more than it cost to produce them. Their hard work and perseverance (surviving the 1890s) seemed to finally pay off. For this generation and those after it, this became the almost mythical benchmark for farming success. Farmers experienced true profits and realized an excellent return on investment. Farmers now defined success as a level of profit "on par" with the profits and prices of 1919, (and on "par" with the profits from non-farm industrial sectors) and the concept of "parity" was born.

Using 1919 as the standard, successful farm policy of the future became policy that gave farmers prices at "parity" with those experienced during these years. The economists will tell you it just couldn't last, that the prices were the result of unique world need that quickly went away when production ramped up elsewhere. But the farmers at the time could not believe it. The post-war consumer boom of the Roaring Twenties made the good times seem like a given, and, as the decade progressed, they were everywhere but on the farm. By 1921, prices had fallen back to pre-war levels and farmers were left behind and wondering what happened to those good old days. As Chapter Three discussed, the political system responded with offers to help the economically suffering farmers, ultimately culminating in the price support policies of New Deal, *twelve* years later. As Chapter Three also notes, the "villain" in the story was President Calvin Coolidge, standing on economic principles and the recognition that artificially propping up of prices was unsustainable in the long haul. The "heroes" were the bi-partisan members of the Senate Farm Bloc, especially the Republicans who defied party leaders to vote for federal farm support. In 1932, Franklin Delano Roosevelt's election finally gave farmers the support they were seeking and modern federal farm assistance was born.

Blue times, Blue Team: FDR and the New Deal

When Franklin Delano Roosevelt introduced his New Deal in 1933, everyone was hurting in the Great Depression. The previous decade had brought a particular stress to farmers, and prices for crops were quite low compared to everything else. This meant the farmer had no money and most everyday items were priced higher than ever—exacerbating the pain. The New Deal's solution was to "fix" the price of farm commodities. This created a dilemma for the Red Team. Republicans were working hard to resist the New Deal at every turn. But they were also aware that their strongest, most reliable fan base was out in the country. They needed the farm vote to keep at least part of the team in Congress at all.

The blue team actually helped them out by choosing to pursue a policy with red team roots. Democrats revived the old vetoed *McNary-Haugen* government purchase program along with price fixing—government set prices for farm products. Republicans went along because McNary and Haughten of the 1920s wore the red jersey, making it an acceptable play for a red team. But they did not stop there. According to congressional scholar and historian Hansen, the red team tried to *outdo* the blue team on farm support. Hansen notes the parties actually appeared to be in a "bidding war" to see who could do more for the farmer.[13] Republicans seemed willing to promise farm groups higher price guarantees than the Democrats—so that at least some of their fans would keep coming to the games. Republicans and Democrats also represented different geographic farm products—corn in the Midwest and cotton, tobacco in the South. The parochialism makes perfect sense when we consider how desperately the Red team needed Red fans in the 1930's. Most of the nation had gone blue. Congress was blue. The President was blue—and would be reelected a record four times. Republicans were clearly on the defensive.

Agricultural policy, even as a "welfare" policy, was focused on the prices of farm products and the problems of commercial farmers. The logic was to help farm families and the farm economy and, by extension, rural areas by increasing the prices farmers received for their products. This, in turn, would help the rural economies which depended on the farm dollar to buy groceries, machinery, labor, and other inputs. In the Senate, farm state Republicans tended to protect the Agricultural Adjustment Acts from Eastern Republicans, who were trying to derail the New Deal at every turn. As anticipated, parochial needs were put above conservative or liberal principles for rural representatives, making them effectively players for the other team.

Many of them may have felt times were desperate and the measures were temporary. However, like most social welfare programs, termination was not on the table when prosperity returned. The Republicans on the Agricultural Committees simply had no stomach for discontinuing farm relief. When World War II lifted farm prices, the members of the House Agricultural Committee remained committed to protecting farm programs in a bipartisan manner forming what thereinafter became referred to as the Farm Bloc.[14] As Hansen notes "The New Deal institutionalized demands for farm subsidies...to terminate it would precipitate economic and political disaster."[15] This is true of most social welfare programs—rent subsidies, food stamps, and student loans included. Entire economies develop in the new (artificial) market structure. To remove the program would be to dismantle the economy of those programs—with both beneficiaries and businesses losing out.

1947 Red Team Rising

As stories go, it's about time for a villain to spoil all this fun—that villain is going to be wearing a *blue* jersey and he is going to make the mistake of making a play for the other team's fans. By 1947, the Feds had literally changed the farm economy, and some farmers realized they weren't necessarily doing better with high prices. That is because the federal policy *also* subjected farmers to strict production controls—they were only allowed to grow so much. Under the old AAA, local Farm Service Agencies dictated the amounts of corn, tobacco, cotton, etc. each grower could plant. In return, farmers were offered programs to help them reach 100% of parity with the prices of the good old days in 1919. However, the policy had lost some of its charm for corn farmers. Post-war prosperity among American consumers was boosting demand for meat, which meant it was boosting demand for corn-fed meat. Corn farmers were doing the math, and they figured out they could make more money if they were allowed to farm more land, even at lower prices. Corn farmers were also concentrated in the Midwest, a red team stronghold. President Truman, a Democrat, wondered if maybe he could win some support in the Midwest and reduce the costs of farm programs, and he announced a plan to offer "flexible price supports" of only 60-90% parity in exchange for release from production controls. This would also have the effect of reducing federal payments and alleviating some pressure on the war-deficit budget.

Even though this idea went against Democratic propensities to hold the line on New Deal programs, Truman wasn't necessarily a turncoat. He was actually playing to win. Democrats had controlled Congress and the Presidency for seven straight elections 1932-1944. (Talk about being the reigning champs!) Then, suddenly, for non-farm reasons, the nation voted in 1946 to give the House and the Senate to the Republicans. This put the Republicans in the unique position of chairing congressional committees implementing New Deal programs, especially the Ag committee. The new team in charge did not want to jeopardize their surprise win by compromising voter programs, especially among their fan base in rural areas, so they planned to stay with 100 % parity. Hansen's analysis of Congressional proceedings of the time showed a Committee leadership that "shunned" partisanship.[16] Rural Republicans and Rural Democrats felt the same— they wanted to protect the farmer. To Washington insiders the bipartisan Farm Bloc seemed alive and well, despite shifts in partisan fortunes. Many also thought the Republicans would continue to dominate rural districts.

But Truman had other ideas. His uncharacteristic offering of flexible price supports precipitated an unprecedented partisan agricultural fight in Congress. According to Hansen, the House Committee, Truman, and USDA Secretary Freeman all supported the new flexible price supports, in part to balance the books and in part to free-up the economy. This made them the enemy of most non-corn farmers who could not make up the lost income in market share. Democrats in the Senate, with more ties to non-corn farmers and an inclination to protect New Deal programs, amended the bill to rigid 90% price supports in a party-line Democratic vote. In a fantastic outcome, the Blue team was able to have it both ways. Some farmers supported Truman while others supported the Senate Democrats. Either way it translated into political support.

In a surprise win, Truman, the Democrat in 1948 defeated the heavily-favored challenger, Republican Thomas Dewey, largely on the farm vote. Remember, the red team was rising—they were supposed to win in a nation tired of New Deal control and ready for more freedom from government dictates. Democrats also took 30 house seats in the Midwest and nine Senate seats, and Congress in both chambers was again controlled by the Democrats by January 1949. Democrats seemed to offer farmers what they wanted, with the President catering to the Midwest and the Senate protecting everyone else. Farm fans looked at the position of the blue players and they liked what they saw. Some saw the President offering corn farmers more profit. Others saw the Democrats in the Senate protecting New Deal programs which had served a generation.

However, once the spell of the AAA had been broken, the two political parties saw an opportunity to use tailored farm programs to obtain pinpointed votes—leading to a severe breakdown in the Farm Bloc. The farm vote could be won or lost with program tinkering, and farmers would simply vote for the team package that offered the most promise for their bottom line. But, USDA secretaries don't think about votes. They think about budgets and programs, and Truman's own USDA secretary spoiled all the fun for the blue team. While the parties were thinking about winning elections and competing for votes, Brannan had his eye on something else. In 1949, Secretary Brannan recognizing the potential of a plurality of programs, proposed to tinker further with farm prices, developing a two tier farm price support program—rigid supports via loan rates and storage for commodities and direct payments for perishables such as milk, eggs, and livestock. Farmers did not like the idea of direct payments, since they would depend on annual appropriations every year, putting them at the mercy of politics at a whole new level. The policy became reviled as the Brannan Plan— and in the 1950 midterm elections, the farm vote punished the blue team. Democrats lost 28 seats in the House and six seats in the Senate. According to Hansen, some farm groups called the Democrat plan "socialism." Democrats took their defeat to heart and worked hard to distance themselves from the reviled Brennan Plan, promising to protect rigid support for farmers. As might be expected, Brannan was kicked off the team, too.

True Competition, True Colors

The development of a new policy, the idea that farm price support did not have to be fixed, created new positions and new plays for each team. On one side was the Blue Team, Democrats, supported by the progressive farm group, National Farmers Union and the Grange. This team argued for rigid price support for farm products and strong federal participation in the farm economy. The NFU is still active today, with the same progressive agenda to protect farm profits using federal programs. The Grange is less of a political organization, but still an active fraternal organization, especially for farm youth. In the stands, rooting for the Blue Team were tobacco and cotton farmers of the South and wheat farmers from the Northern tier of the Great Plains. The South and North Great Plains had a long history of supporting the Blue team anyway. The South was reliably Democrat since the time of the civil war. The North Great Plains was home of the old Populist party of the 1890s. Both were looking for a party to protect them from the capitalist acumen of the Republican Party.

On the other side was the Red Team, Republicans, supported by the corn-belt dominated American Farm Bureau. This team argued for flexible price support, lower federal expenditures and more free market farm decisions. In the stands, rooting for the Red Team were the corn growers of the Midwest. The Midwest along with the North East had kept the Red Team on the field during the Blue team-dominant years of New Deal politics. Political scientist, Adam Sheingate notes that the issue of rigid or flexible price support kept farmers from becoming a reliable constituency of either party. While other nations have one party that supports farmers and one organization that fights for farmers, the United States has a plurality of farm groups and farm politicians—and this led to interesting political fights in the post-New Deal world.

Foxes in the Henhouse

Eisenhower and Ezra Taft Benson: Paring Down Parity

At the same time, both teams were populated by rogue players who took the game too far and angered the fan base. First there was Eisenhower, playing for the red team in 1953. He had won office with a half-hearted promise maintain farm programs. However, he appointed an economic conservative, Ezra Taft Benson, as USDA secretary to do his dirty work and undermine farm program support. Like good Republicans, they wanted less government and more free-market forces in the farm economy. Economic conservatives do not typically support social welfare policies, and now one was the leader of a sizeable program, with predictable results. Secretary Benson tried to shame farmers into seeing themselves as welfare recipients: "Farmers should not be placed in a position of working for government bounty rather than producing for a free market."[17] He set out to dismantle government price control of agriculture products, and he wanted to get the government out of the unprofitable business of paying farmers high prices for products the government had to sell or destroy at a loss.

As a shrewd player of politics, Secretary Benson realized he could invite an entirely new set of fans, much larger than the farm vote, to root for the red team's free market policies. Consumers were paying high prices for staples such as butter, bread and milk *because of* government price programs. To gain the attention of these fans, especially housewives, he had the USDA publish the cost of the farm program on the price of groceries. He also lifted the curtain on shameful USDA practices of destroying farm products, even livestock, to keep prices high for farmers. The savvy publication of these practices had the predictable result of increasing citizen scrutiny of farm programs and farm spending.

Secretary Benson used this political momentum to push for flexible farm support in Congress as a way to free up resources. He is credited as the first person to use the term "freedom to farm" as a rally cry to reduce federal planting restrictions and allow farmers to choose less government support ("Flexible" support) in exchange for less government say in the fields.[18] Because you cannot dismantle any welfare program overnight, requests in Congress were modest. Teammates in red jerseys offered an amendment to move farm support from 90% parity to 82.5% parity, setting the stage for a red team/blue team showdown on farm support policy. With such a program in play, the teams showed their true colors.[19] Almost all of the red players (88%) voted for reduced farm supports. Almost all of the blue players (76%) voted to keep high farm supports. This set up a pattern in the 1950's of Democrats holding the line on rigid support, and it led to expected electoral gains in areas dependent on federal farm programs. Republicans continued to advocate for flexible supports, on the principle of reduced government spending in the farm sector.

These team strategies were not lost on the original fans in the stands. Additional farmers came out for the blue team. By 1958, Democrats were even winning Midwestern congressional seats from wheat farming areas. Commentators tend to characterize this as the beginning of commodity politics, with farmers splitting according to the market advantages of federal policy and *their* product. As might be expected, the teams could no longer claim to speak for the farmer in general. Indeed, future farm policy will begin to fragment into separate policies for separate farm products in an attempt to please the increasingly fragmented farm vote. During this time, the American Farm Bureau (AFB), led by an Iowa corn farmer, was solidly conservative and became a loyal sponsor of the Red team, advocating for flexible price supports.

To veteran farm policy watchers these developments were troubling. Farm policy had been predictably controlled by a bipartisan farm bloc, doling out goodies to each region and each commodity. Now the players found they were no longer able or allowed to huddle together and move their ball down the field in unison. Instead, they had to start playing for their respective teams again to maintain their position on the team. Some contemporaries of the time truly lamented the loss of bipartisanship in farm policy.[20] Other commentators praised the new found competition in the sport as a way to break up the powerful farm bloc and its commitment to producer-oriented food policy.[21] They wanted a national policy focused on the rest of the nation and its needs. "What about the rest of us?" became a common sentiment and rally cry among those not in the farm bloc.

Kennedy and Freeman, Policing Planting

The second rogue player on the scene played for the blue team. The Democrats had just managed to wrestle a great deal of the farm vote from Republican strongholds, but their new President did not understand the need to tread lightly. President Kennedy and his USDA Secretary Orville Freeman, upon regaining control of the ball, attempted an even more radical move in the other direction, reminding farmers of the downside of generous Democratic programs— production control. Kennedy advocated for a new "supply management policy" with very strict production controls and criminal-like policing for farmers who planted more than they were allotted by their local agencies. This plan was characterized as practically communist by the AFB as a plan for "food produced by docile, licensed and properly managed farmers."[22] When it was included in the Farm Bill, even Democrats balked at supporting it. In 1962, there was unified Republican opposition to the farm bill, with even a few southern Democrats joining them. The midterm elections punished Democrats for Kennedy's strict production controls and Republicans retook Midwestern House seats.

The Return of the Bipartisan Huddle: Voluntary Programs

After the Kennedy-Freeman fiasco, Democrats on the Agriculture Committee knew they needed a fresh start. The old way of supporting farmers by guaranteeing price and controlling supply just wasn't going to work fiscally or politically. The rigid price supports were not only costly in elections, but were also expensive for taxpayers and difficult to justify to consumers concerned about high food prices. Since the Red Team seemed to have the momentum, some of these blue players decided to look at the Republican playbook and consider huddling together again. Earlier in the year, a South Dakota Republican Senator had floated the idea of a voluntary wheat certification program rather than strict production limits under penalty of prosecution. The idea was to offer more generous price supports to farmers who would limit production *voluntarily*. Democrats now seized on the innovative idea of *voluntary* programs as a new way out. Hansen notes that the innovative concept was political genius for two reasons: "First, it removed the most objectionable part of the program."[23] It also "invited cooperation from across the aisle."

Farm Bloc Republicans were willing to go along. Similar to the old *McNary-Haugen* call for cooperation, this idea originated with a member of their own party. Furthermore, their main election issue with farmers had been the heavy hand of federal production controls. This policy innovation removed that objectionable coercion from the federal farm program. Voluntary farm programs were *bipartisan* farm programs once again, with congressional committee members cooperating in the huddle once again. Republicans actually proposed an old Truman Administration idea of direct payments—the most welfare-like program yet—rather than supporting prices by buying farmer's surplus at parity prices. The 1965 farm bill received significant Republican support for the first time since 1954, and bipartisan cooperation became the norm again on farm programs. Even so, plenty of other players were not happy about these defections, and members in the huddle knew their real enemies to be members of their own team.

---

[1] The use of the term hero or villain is not meant to signal support or detraction for the policy. If one is a free market advocate and skeptical of social welfare programs, those players and teams opposing federal farm and food programs would certainly be heroes—and those protecting them, especially in defiance of their own team—would certainly be villains. Because farm policy was originally conceptualized as helping farmers, I have chosen to phrase the hero/villain discussion accordingly. I fully expect some readers to root for the villains instead of the heroes.

[2] According to scholars and policymakers, food and agriculture policy is overwhelmingly considered bipartisan due to its locally-focused, log-rolling and distributive nature (Mercier 2011, Gilbert an Oladi, 2010, Hurwitz, Moiles, Rohde 2001, Lee 2008). In terms of geography, agriculture interests were historically widely dispersed across the majority of geographically based Congressional districts. As late as 1950, two-thirds of American counties were "farming dependent" (Mercier 2011) having at least 15% of residents' earnings or employment arising from the agricultural sector. In terms of logrolling, agriculture policy was the poster-child exemplar of members without anything in common trading votes, by incorporating the Food Stamp program (a poverty program disproportionately benefiting urban districts) into the Farm Bill, which was mostly an agriculture and rural development bill (Abler 1989, Outlaw, Richardson & Klose 2011). In terms of distributive politics, distributive programs have broad costs and concentrated benefits—such as farm subsidies and rural development grants—and these tend to ordinarily pass by consensus (Weingast 1979) because they directly benefit constituents (Lowi 1964). Scholars of farm policy have found evidence of bipartisan, distributive voting (Hurwitz, Moiles, and Rohde 2001; Lee 2008; Odum 2012). In terms of farm commodity programs, Sheingate (2001) notes that parties used to exploit economic zero-sum policies among producers of different commodities to capture (partisan) votes. However, after 1965, that source of economic conflict went away with individual commodity programs (one for wheat, one for cotton, one for sugar, one for milk) and individual commodity lobbies (who could work with either party). Scholars attribute voluntary and individual commodity programs with finding bi-partisanship among members of Congress 1960-1980, and less than one-third of roll call votes on agriculture were partisan during this period (Sheingate 2001). For this part of the debate, even recent scholars still refer to agriculture as the "quieter milieu" in terms of partisan conflict (Krutz 2005).

[3] Historians refer to this as the classical liberalism of American society—a belief independence, liberty, and capitalism. Louis Hartz famously noted that America had no feudalistic society, making it much less attracted to socialism. (Louis Hartz. 1955. The Liberal Tradition in America: An Interpretation of American Political Thought Since the Revolution. New York: Houghton Mifflin Harcourt). There was no expectation that a king or governor or President would come to your aid on the frontier or in the city—at least not until the Great Depression and the New Deal.

[4] Sheingate, Adam D. 2001. *The Rise of the Agriculture Welfare State*. Princeton University Press. p. 1

[5] Sheingate, 2001, p. 1

[6] Critics of farm policy on the liberal side usually question the fact that the policy disproportionately benefits large corporate-like operations. Very contemporary liberal critics also question the public health and environmental consequences of commodity-based farm policy, feeling that social welfare policy should go further to ensure healthy outcomes for the nation as a whole. Critics on the left and the right have also argued against policies that raise prices for the consumer.

[7] Novak, James, James W. Pease and Larry D. Sanders. 2015. *Agricultural Policy in the United States: Evolution and Economics*. New York: Routledge. p. 4.

[8] Forest Laws. 2017. "Health care battle may presage next farm bill debate" Southeast Farm Press. May 3, 2017. p. 4.

[9] ibid

[10] Jose A. DelReal. 2017. "Trump seeks 4.7 billion in Cuts to USDA Discretionary Spending." *The Washington Post*. March 16, 2017. https://www.washingtonpost.com/national/trump-seeks-47-billion-in-cuts-to-usda-discretionary-spending/2017/03/15/c8fd5622-09ab-11e7-b77c-0047d15a24e0_story.html?utm_term=.6d93f7fa179a

[11] Progressive farming guru, Joel Salatin of Polyface farm, made this sentiment famous with his best-selling book *Everything I want to do is Illegal: War Stories from the Local Food Front*. Chelsea Green Publishing. 2007.

[12] Smith, Robert C. and Richard A. Seltzer. 2015. *Polarization and the Presidency: From FDR to Barak Obama*. Boulder, CO: Lynne Rienner Publishers.

[13] Hansen pp. 90-92.

[14] For an readable and entertaining ntroduction to Washington politics and the early farm bloc see journalist Wesley McCune. 1943. *The Farm Bloc*. Garden City, NY: Doubleday, Doran and Company, Inc.

[15] Hansen p. 97.

[16] Hansen p. 91

[17] Sheingate p. 134

[18] Hansen p. 136

[19] Pennock, J. Roland. 1956. "Party and constituency in postwar agricultural price support legislation." *Journal of Politics* 18:171-181 (May 1956)

[20] Sheingate p. 139 quoting Kiplinger,s Washington Letter, February 1, 1958, "Farm state congressmen can't get a bill through Congress. The Farm Bloc in the old days always stood together. Now it has internal quarrels, so [there is] a stalemate."

[21] Lowi, Theodore J. 1964. "How the farmers get what they want," *Reporter* May 21, 1964 pp. 34-37.

[22] Hansen p. 148

[23] Hansen p. 153

Chapter 5

Conservative Backlash and Contemporary Politics

As we have seen so far, we have a bi-partisan farm bloc, periodically torn apart by electoral prospects and radical partisan ideas from presidential leaders. We also have a unique geography of the farm vote and attempts to regain the White House or Congress by using the farm vote as a chessboard for a winning coalition. Things are about to change as the Republican critique of progressivism gains its footing in politics.

Contemporary Conservatism and Red Team Opposition to Farm Programs

Chairman Reagan and the Rebirth of Conservatism

Waiting in the wings of the red team was an orator who could put just the right touch on the problem with welfare, especially farm welfare. In 1964, former actor Ronald Reagan made a televised speech specifically targeting farm programs to lay out the promise of conservative ideology and conservative candidates. Reagan was serving as California Co-chair for Republican presidential candidate Barry Goldwater. He wanted to lay out the promise of conservatism as an anecdote for wasteful and inefficient government policies. His object of choice was the federal farm program and the Washington Post called the broadcast speech a "barn burner."[1] Reagan's position was the superiority of the free market in efficient resource allocation versus the terrible track record of government regulation of farming. After making the case for private sector free market control of the economy, Reagan went on to skewer modern farm policy as exhibition #1 of inefficient government economic meddling:

> Now, we have no better example of this than government's involvement in the farm economy over the last thirty years. Since 1955, the cost of this program has nearly doubled. One fourth of farming in America is responsible for 85% of the [persistently problematic] farm surplus. Three-fourths of farming is out on the free market and has known a 21% increase in the per capita consumption of its produce. You see, that one-fourth of farming-that's regulated and controlled by the federal government. Senator Humphrey [D-Minn.] last week charged that a Barry Goldwater presidency would seek to eliminate farmers. He should do his homework a little better, because he'll find out that we've had a decline of 5 million in the farm population under these government programs. He'll also find that the Democratic Administration [Kennedy's plan] has sought to get from Congress [an] extension of the farm program to include the three-fourths that is now free. He'll find they've also asked for the right to imprison farmers who would not keep books as proscribed by the Federal Government. The Secretary of Agriculture [Freeman] asked for the right to seize farms through condemnation and resell them to other individuals. And, contained in that same program was a provision that would have allowed the federal government to remove two million farmers from the soil. At the same time, there has been an increase in the Department of Agriculture employees. Every responsible farmer and farm organization has repeatedly asked for the government to free the farm economy, but how are farmers to know what's best for them? The wheat farmers voted against a wheat program [Farm Bureau Federated Vote]. The government passed it anyway. Now the price of bread goes up and the price of wheat to the farmer goes down.[2]

Reagan made several interesting points in this speech. While it is famous among political historians for galvanizing the modern conservative movement, few know that it was about food policy. First, Reagan blamed the surpluses on government programs that created artificial incentives to over produce. As he rightly notes, most of farming, especially the fruit and vegetable growing in California, is done without subsides—and is done more efficiently with no wasteful and price gouging surpluses. Second, Reagan appeals to civil liberties in his condemnation of federal police action against *farmers* for *farming*. What could be criminal about a pastoral, independent, hardworking profession? Third, he appeals to democratic self-rule and notes that even the Farm Bloc's bipartisan huddle seems out-of-touch with the farmers themselves.

Ronald Reagan went on to become Governor of California in 1967 and President of the U.S. in 1981. As with Coolidge and Eisenhower, new generation

Republican Presidents began to lament the lack of free market principles in the Farm Bill. In 1972, Nixon campaigned on ending farm programs but, as Hansen notes, there was a gentleman's agreement in Congress to protect farm programs: "No one took Nixon's plan to phase out farm programs seriously."[3] Bipartisan congressional support for farm programs was ascendant, and the farm bloc team huddle closed ranks to protect its prerogatives.

Reagan maintained his opposition to the farm bill as President throughout the 1980's. When he signed the 1981 Farm Bill early in his term, he noted that "returning to the principles of free enterprise will return us all to prosperity."[4] After reelection, he pursued these values more vigorously. During the devastating farm crisis of the period when 30% of farms were vulnerable to foreclosure in Iowa, and farm corporations were circling to buy the discounted farms, Reagan *vetoed* the Farm Bill. In March 1985 he is quoted in the Chicago Tribune saying "The government cannot bail out every farmer hopelessly in debt."[5] The Tribune went on to say the bill had passed Congress because "few lawmakers wanted to be on record against aid when so many farmers are facing desperate financial problems."[6] In his Oval Office speech defending the veto, Reagan said, "Someone must be willing to stand up for those who pay America's bills…Someone must stand up to those who say 'take as many hard earned tax dollars as you want.' "[7] Democrats were hoping to make inroads into 35 Republican held districts considered vulnerable, and Reagan's veto gave the blue team a rural campaign issue. In an interesting twist, however, *urban* Democrats sided with Reagan to support further farm cuts.[8] Urban Democrats were not particularly concerned with welfare for farmers.

However, as we have seen before, hard times can make even the most conservative red player sympathetic or at least politically motivated to help the farmer. The veto that seemed so right in March seemed heartless in the post-harvest season of the American holidays. Farm prices were so low (due to that old enemy *surplus*) that farmers could not pay their bills and were being turned out of their generational homes. Reagan did what any Santa Claus would do and signed a farm bill, the Food Security Act of 1985, in December. He defended his turnabout with the following statements:

> This legislation reauthorizes virtually all of our farm programs. Today farmers and ranchers are currently suffering through difficult times. These difficulties have been caused in part by the very same government programs that were designed to help American agriculture. Earlier this year, my administration proposed a market-oriented farm bill designed to correct past farm policies that have often worked at cross-purposes. We have encouraged farmers to produce more commodities by artificially propping up prices while, at the same time, forcing farmers to set aside more and more land to reduce production so that prices would not drop. As a result of such counterproductive farm policies, the American farmer

has become less competitive in the international market place, the cost of our farm programs has risen to unsustainable levels, and farm income has become stagnated.[9]

After noting a few reforms he wanted, such as reduced price support to make exports competitive and decoupled payments to remove incentives to overproduce, Reagan went on to criticize the bill, even as he signed it: "By failing to totally uncouple farm income support from planting decisions, and by keeping support prices artificially high, we will encourage more and more farmers to become dependent upon our farm programs. These programs represent the worst in the way of policy."[10] Because the bill did somewhat lower price supports and did somewhat discourage overproduction, Reagan signed it as a "step in the right direction."

The LA Times declared the next day "Reagan signs History's Most Costly Farm Bill."[11] Members of Congress facing a year of very sympathetic news coverage for farmers and hurting rural communities, as they did in the 1930s, sought to do more, regardless of party. However, fiscal reality set in and the 1990 farm bill continued to face conservative opposition. According to Hansen "the farm bloc accepted even deeper cuts in conference, as part of the 1990 budget accord, rather than throw the bill open on the floor."[12]

The Other Welfare Policy: Food Stamps, Consumers and Team Politics

Recall, however, that farmers are not the only fans in the stands. Voters in the cities and suburbs had their own concerns when it comes to food policy, and the voting power of consumers began to take on new meaning. During the 1970's American Consumerism was the latest liberal reform movement, and a number of measures were passed to protect consumers from producers, particularly with regard to product safety.[13] However, inflation led to high retail food prices, generating "unprecedented public scrutiny of the Federal Government in Agricultural price making."[14] Consumerism also had a geographic component to politics. Since most food consumers live in the cities, this gave urban representatives an incentive to get involved in agriculture policy, and many of them wore the blue jersey. With blue players concerned about food prices, red players critical of farm spending saw the chance to huddle with their opponents. In this spirit, some Republicans began to court urban and suburban lawmakers to "abolish these programs which inflate the price of our food."[15] Even today, the conservative Republican Freedom Caucus sought to derail farm programs by working with members of the *blue* team in 2014 and 2018.

Welfare for farmers is one thing. Welfare for the poor is another, when it comes to team politics. The biggest political change in Farm Policy was its marriage to poverty policy during the Great Society—a next generation New Deal policy. By the 1970s, aid to the poor now included special food dollars called food stamps. What started in 1939-1943 as a pilot program was included, but not implemented in 1958 and finally expanded Kennedy in 1964. Congress put the USDA food stamp program into the Farm Bill as a "logroll" between Southern members supporting farm programs and urban liberals who wanted nutrition subsidies. By 1973, the Farm Bill formally included the Food Stamp Act in the nutrition title (along with other USDA programs such as WIC, school lunch and TEPAF) to authorize direct payments from the USDA to low-income households to buy food. That year the Food Stamp program was expanded to garner urban votes. This had the permanent effect of creating a "log roll" where rural representatives would support urban poverty programs in exchange for urban votes for farm programs. Logroll is the term used when members with little in common (such as rural versus urban) support each other's policy needs. Not all players supported the USDA food stamp program. Southern Democrats and Midwestern Republicans remained hostile to the new urban liberalism of Great Society programs including food dollars for the poor.[16] However, the majority of the nation was pretty much on board. A 1968 CBS special *Hunger in America* created a new public awareness of hunger issues, generating additional public concern about food relief. In 1973 the House and Senate Agriculture Committees incorporated the food stamp program into the farm bill, and 1975 spending on food stamp entitlements surpassed federal spending on farm programs. By 2014, 85 % of Farm Bill spending would be for food stamps, by then renamed the Supplemental Nutrition Assistance Program. With this modern hybrid farm bill, many urban blue players could vote for the farm bill and tell their fans they were voting for anti-poverty programs.

1996 Freedom to Farm: Conservatives Storm the Barn

All of these programs cost money, and by the 1990s conservative criticism of government deficit spending was reaching a clamor. In 1994, Republicans took over both houses of Congress for the first time in 30 years, and House Republicans elected a firebrand Speaker of the House, Newt Gingrich. The red team was more ideological (conservative) in its purported goals for the nation, especially with regard to government spending and government interference in the free market economy. Both of these goals put farm subsidy programs squarely in their crosshairs for elimination. Sheingate claims the budgetary impact of commodity support programs, which were largely in the shape of direct payments to farmers, was the key political concern, especially when government was borrowing to pay its bills.[17]

The red team's "Contract with America" promised to balance the federal budget, but the politics for individual Republicans in Congress where tricky. Rural districts had voted in the Republicans, and were generally more conservative on most government policy. However, some of those fans supported farm programs.

Sheingate notes that 35 House Republicans represented districts where "at least 5% of the population was employed by agriculture".[18] Sheingate further notes that forty-three percent of freshmen House members had "significant agricultural activity" in their districts.[19] In effect, Congressmen had to weigh whether they thought the agriculture vote would switch to Democratic support in the next election. Even more interesting is the continued conservatism of the American Farm Bureau and its continued support for free market principles.

Like the Democrats in the 1950s, the Republicans began to search for a way to cut farm programs while retaining farm votes. As with earlier evolutions in farm support policy, one plan rose to the top. While the Senate produced a plan with severe, yet complicated cuts for commodity supports, the House won the day with a simpler approach. As Sheingate notes:

> House Agricultural Chairman Pat Roberts introduced a more radical proposal that would eliminate all acreage controls and price supports linked to production, including target prices and deficiency payments. Instead, farmers would receive 'market transition payments' that would be phased out over the next seven years. Politically, the Roberts proposal—otherwise known as the Freedom to Farm plan—gained support over other proposals because it cut costs, simplified regulations, and most important, was easy to grasp by non-specialists. In the words of a senior Republican staff member in the House Agriculture Committee, 'We have come up with a farm policy people understand.' These qualities made the Roberts plan an immediate favorite among the House leadership and the Republican rank and file."[20]

But, Sheingate documents, Republicans on the House Agricultural Committee were not so sure. As before, Midwest corn and soybean districts favored the free-market approach while Southern cotton and rice districts did not. In the Committee vote, four Republicans joined the Democrats to defeat the bill. Most of these Democrats were Southerners defending government support for farmers. However, House leadership was not deterred and simply placed Freedom to Farm in the budget bill. For non-farm reasons, President Clinton, a Democrat, vetoed the budget bill leading to an impasse between him and Congress that shut down federal government operations in 1995. However, the teams had clearly staked out new territory in farm policy. According to Sheingate, all involved understood that House Republican Leadership did not "care" about agriculture and that they had successfully wrestled control for agriculture policy from the more bipartisan insiders of the Agricultural committee. The teams had also solidified their new fans in the stands. Politically, this farm bill was about taxpayers, consumers and environmentalists—everyone but the farmer—constituencies with much broader appeal. Taxpayer issues were a core issue of the Republicans and those fans saw the red team best suited to tackle the issue of runaway government spending.

Consumer and environmental issues were core issues for urban and suburban Democrats. This left only a few parochially placed members of both teams, mostly farm district blue players, to support high commodity payments to farmers. On the other hand, many farmers did not see Newt Gingrich as a villain at all. They wanted the "freedom to farm" and supported less government intervention overall. They also supported lower taxes and less government programs in general, especially urban poverty programs.

President Clinton ultimately signed the 1996 Farm Bill praising it for freeing farmers to "plant for the market, not for government programs."[21] However, in a characteristically ideological note, he stated, "I am signing H.R. 2854 with reservation because I believe the bill fails to provide an adequate safety net for family farms." Indeed in the 1996 farm bill was a partisan vote in the House with Republicans voting yea 216 (19 nay) and Democrats voting Nay 136 (54 yea). Notable parochial interests dominated cross-party voting for this bill. Democrats and Republicans from the South and other farming areas voted for the bill *against* their party.[22] The Senate version was passed by a voice vote, so there is no record of party voting on this bill.

21ˢᵗ Century Farm Bills: Same ole, Same ole

A Modern Farm Bill

By 2002, the plot had again become fairly predictable. Republicans want to cut farm programs unless times are really bad. Then, like Reagan before them, they will find their mantle of compassionate conservatism and buy the farmers a little more time. This is exactly what happened in 2002. As with the 1920's, export markets dried up, partly from new competition for grains and beef from South America. These lost sales dramatically lowered commodity prices triggering higher direct payments for farmers. (The same thing will happen after the 2014 farm bill.) Where Congress had hoped to make farm prices more dependent on the free market, the tough times of market-oriented farm prices were difficult to swallow politically. Many benefits cut in 1996 were restored in the 2002 farm bill and good economic times for the rest of the country made budget concerns less of an issue. In comparing the change of heart from 1996 to 2002, Economist Ronald Knutson offers a nice summary of the partisan approaches of the time:

> The 1996 farm bill was based on the value judgment that government spending on agriculture needed to be more predictable each year and reduced over time. Budget issues were front and center in that farm bill debate. In contrast, the 2002 farm bill was passed following several years of budget surpluses, and spending issues were less of a consideration, enabling open-ended entitlements to be enhanced.[23]

Knutson goes on to explain that red team, blue team competition in farm policy was the new normal, with a Democratic farm bill from the Senate and a Republican farm bill from the House, much like 2014.[24]

Much of the farm bill debate that sits in the mind of today's players originated in 2002. Of issue was the fact that the bulk of direct payments were now understood to go to the largest agricultural operations, not small family farms. Also, many more conservatives, who generally counted on the farm vote, also came to understand the market-distorting and budget busting propensities of a subsidized farm program. This created quite a conflict between parochial needs and ideological principles for members of the red team. For the blue team, those sympathetic to farmers justified market intervention with the idea that the market failed to adequately reward farmers.

The 2002 Farm bill also strengthened environmental cost-share programs first enacted in 1996 to help farmers implement conservation practices. These voluntary programs offer to cover a portion of the costs of environmental upgrades on the farm or offer to pay rent for ground set aside for conservation or wildlife habitat. These programs also tended to benefit larger producers, such as those with expansive feedlots or farms with large acreage. The idea of using government largess to assist these corporate-like agricultural operations also created interesting partisan sentiments. Republicans generally supported the program, expecting government to lessen the impact of environmental regulations by making them voluntary and less costly for business. Democrats often felt the money should not go to large operations with expensive projects and upgrades, but saw the value of renting ground to keep it out of production.

By 2002, there is also an increasing recognition of the environmental footprint of agriculture, with predictable partisan results. Democrats see agriculture as an industry to be held accountable for its pollution the same as any other industry. Republicans see onerous environmental compliance as a drag on productivity, especially for those in small business, like most farmers. This is why voluntary environmental programs became the norm for agriculture in the farm bill. To force more environmental compliance Democratic administrations and the EPA would also work with regional authorities, such as the Chesapeake Bay initiative, to find additional ways to regulate agricultural environmental outputs. For example, the EPA started to regulate water run-off from farming operations, like poultry houses. One conundrum is the fact that involuntary environmental compliance is least costly for large organizations with economies of scale. The small family farm has a much more difficult time building costly structures and practices into its operation at a profitable level. Furthermore, the paper work and required documentation upkeep can bury a family operation while large operations often have designated staff for compliance issues or hire third parties to take care of them. The increase of rigid environmental regulation under later Democratic administrations made many agricultural producers fans of the red team, even if the red team did not support subsidies. This is especially true because most producers must deal with environmental regulation while only some participate in subsidy programs. The red team's general stance of reduced federal regulation of any kind (including labor and taxation) made them an attractive team for the conventional farmer.

Also at issue in 2002 was the renewed interest in the importance of trade to sustained American agricultural growth and profits. Opening new markets became an important goal for commodity and livestock groups, including dairy. The red team generally promotes free trade and this dovetailed nicely with agricultural needs. The blue team, supported by organized labor unions, typically works to protect domestic industry from foreign competition. That said, blue team presidents have fostered their share of free trade agreements, largely to the benefit of agriculture. President Clinton negotiated NAFTA, which expanded corn exports to Mexico and beef exports to Canada. President Obama negotiated the Trans Pacific Partnership and the opening of Cuba, which would have expanded American agriculture access to Asian and Cuban markets. When Trump reversed Obama on Cuba and withdrew from the TPP in 2017, agricultural interests which had supported his presidency, were the first to cry foul. It was an uncharacteristic play by a "red" player, likely due more to his populist (as opposed to conservative) temperament.

A final key component of 2002 "food" policy was not about food at all. The energy title of the farm bill placed a renewed emphasis on homegrown renewable fuels from corn and soybeans. The policy was meant to grow demand for farm products and to lessen American dependence on foreign oil in a post 9/11 world. Today, 40% of the corn crop is used for ethanol, an alternative fuel with the added benefit of burning cleaner. Like trade, the advent of extensive ethanol mandates expanded the demand for corn, initially raising prices and increasing complaints that agricultural programs should grow food, not fuel. As noted at the beginning of this chapter, American food policy is largely about farmers, not consumers. With ethanol, the government is really subsidizing corn production three times over: with direct subsidy payments to growers, with subsidized insurance for commodities, and with mandated use in fuel markets. This artificial market has the added incentive of drawing additional lands and players into the corn market. Prices predictably rose and output predictably increased. Yet, by 2018, farmers will again be complaining of low prices due to a strong dollar (which reduces export demand) and record harvests. This cyclical problem of boom and busts makes contemporary red team, blue team response to farming somewhat idiosyncratic even as both teams try to hold to an ideological and political course.

G. W. Bush Vetoes the Farm Bill?

By 2008, the story line should come as no surprise to us, even though many contemporary commentators were caught off-guard. George W. Bush, a Republican President as ideological as Reagan, *vetoes* the 2008 Farm Bill. Wait a minute—isn't this the Texan cowboy-hat wearing red team captain? How could he veto a farm bill?! Well, for the same reason Reagan did it. He opposed farm subsidies as market distorting tools. He also wanted to cut federal spending. His sign or veto pattern was the reverse of Reagan. In 2002, farmers were hurting and the farm bill was a red team product that reversed many of the "freedom to farm" provisions of the 1996 bill. In 2008, farmers were doing very well, and vulnerable to charges of unnecessary government spending. In this spirit, the Bush Administration lobbied for removing farm subsidies payments for farmers making over $200,000 a year, hoping the red team could begin to reclaim some of the 1996 momentum to wean farmers from government support. [25] Since a small number of large farms receive most of the subsidies, this would have reduced commodity outlays quite a bit and affected most farmers not at all.

It helps to remember that in 2008 the blue team-controlled Congress (Speaker Nancy Pelosi and Senate Majority Leader Harry Reid). The Democrats had taken over Congress in 2007 and were looking forward to more victories in the 2008 election cycle. They hoped that rural-friendly policies might give them an edge in red team districts. Their Farm Bill, while reducing some commodity spending, largely maintained the reinstated programs of 2002. Gone completely was Freedom to farm's promise of phasing out farm subsidies, a cherished conservative position. Furthermore, by 2008, the focus is not on commodities, but on feeding the nation. By this time, 78% of the farm bill spending was for the Supplemental Nutrition Assistance Program (the new name for the food stamp) program. Farm Bills were now called Food bills, with 2008 titled Food, Conservation and Energy Act of 2008. Notice the emphasis on blue team values— food for the citizens and conserving the environment.

The blue team also added quite a bit of new parts to the farm bill. The new food bill included a crop insurance title, horticulture title, organic agriculture provisions and livestock provisions—all policies which had previously been handled with separate bills but were now included to increase support for *this* bill. The new food bill also contained provisions supporting farmers markets, expanding school lunch programs and improving food safety. Some of these provisions helped secure support from a variety of players who otherwise would not care about a farm bill. Some progressive commentators advocated for these policies to move farm support away from health-compromising commodities and towards the consumption of more fruits and vegetables. [26] In fact, congressional support was so great that the House and Senate passed the 2008 food bill over President Bush's veto. The override required a two-thirds vote in each chamber! Pretty impressive. In the House, almost all Democrats supported the bill, but the Republicans were split about half and half.

In his veto remarks, President Bush sounded a lot like the conservatives before him. "At a time of high food prices and record farm income, this bill lacks program reform and fiscal discipline. It continues subsidies for the wealthy and increases farm bill spending by more than $20 billion."[27] Like Reagan, he noted his desire for "more market oriented policies." He goes on to say:

> I veto this bill fully aware that it is rare for a stand-alone farm bill not to receive the President's signature, but my action today is not without precedent. In 1956, President Eisenhower stood firmly on principle, citing high crop subsidies and too much government control of farm programs among the reasons for his veto. President Eisenhower wrote in his veto message, "Bad as some provisions of this bill are, I would have signed it if in total it could be interpreted as sound and good for farmers and the nation." For similar reasons, I am vetoing the bill before me today.[28]

His echoes of Eisenhower's call for "sound" policies continue the thread of Calvin Coolidge's call for a program built on the laws of economics almost eighty years before. As we have already concluded, Presidents on the red team have been fairly consistent in their criticism of farm programs, and sometimes acted accordingly.

What Did President Obama Do?

So what about 2014? What happens when the Red team controls Congress and the Blue team has President Obama? To put it mildly, all heck breaks loose. By the middle of the Obama Administration, the red team is riding a wave of Tea Party and Freedom Caucus backlash against the Affordable Care Act and the opposition party's business as usual approach to compromise. Their fans are literally asking them to quit helping the Democrats move the ball down the field. Caught in the middle of this sentiment is the normally "bipartisan" (Or at least more cooperative) farm bill. While moderate Republicans were prepared to go along, Freedom Caucus Republicans said no way. They want to dismantle the farm bill, with its subsidized farm economy and its massive SNAP program, which has ballooned under generous packages from the Great Recession of 2008-09. The House Freedom Caucus actually succeeds in divorcing the Nutrition Title from the rest of the farm bill, in an attempt to kill it. Their strategy was to target blue team urban players who only support the farm bill because of its poverty programs. By removing the Nutrition Title, these Republicans thought they could remove the necessary Democratic votes for a farm bill. They also thought they could drastically reduce SNAP spending by offering a Nutrition bill that would appeal to a majority of their teammates. It was an ambitious move.

In the end, the farm bloc stuck together, with the few remaining farm state Democrats convincing their teammates to support the farm bill on other merits. The Senate also held the line for them, as discussed in the introduction to this book. The resulting bill had moderate reductions in subsidy programs and nutrition programs, befitting the overall red team flavor of social welfare policies in general.

President Obama's remarks are telling for explaining his support and blue team votes for the farm bill. With high praise for farm state Democratic Senator Debbie Stabenow of Michigan, President Obama explained the social welfare nature of the farm bill. First, he noted, as Sheingate would have anticipated, the farm bill is an income support bill for farmers:

> There are a lot of big producers who are doing really well, but there are even more small farms, family farms, where folks are just scratching out a living and increasingly vulnerable to difficulties in financing and all the inputs involved—farmers sometimes having to work off the farm, they've got a couple of jobs outside the farm just to get healthcare, just to pay the bills, trying to keep it in the family, and it is very hard for young farmers to get started.[29]

In the spirit of a social welfare program, the President described "how hard it can be to be a farmer" with the implication that government should continue to help.

Second, President Obama characterized the bill as "not just about helping farmers" In a laundry list of other blue team policy goals, he explains the merits of the farm bill. "It is a jobs bill, an innovation bill, an infrastructure bill, a research bill, a conservation bill." In his speech he highlighted investment in rural hospitals and schools, affordable housing, broadband infrastructure, biofuels, conservation efforts in the Mississippi River Valley and Chesapeake Bay, local food, farmer's markets, organic agriculture. In terms of programs for farmers, the President emphasized crop insurance, and the reduction in commodity programs: "this bill helps to clamp down on loopholes that allowed people to receive benefits year after year, whether they were planting crops or not making sure that we only support farmers when disaster strikes or prices drop. It is not just automatic." Gone are the days when parity amounts were the stuff of mainstream farm bill politics.

Third, the President spent one-third of his remarks on the farm bill's poverty programs:

> The second thing this farm bill does is help make sure America's children don't go hungry. For more than half a century, this country has helped Americans put food on the table when they hit a rough patch, or when they are working hard but aren't making enough money to feed their kids. That's the idea behind what's known as the Supplemental Nutrition Assistance Program [food stamps]. A large majority of SNAP recipients are children or the elderly or Americans with disabilities.

He also highlighted the nutrition goals of the farm bill for "healthy kids."

With these remarks, the President seemed to pivot from a focus on farmers to a focus on the rest of the nation, especially rural America and needy America. Underlying this is the clear notion that farm policy is social welfare policy—with a broader constituency than "just" farmers. As captain of the blue team, he seems to recognize that the fans in the stands are no longer farmers, but progressives and working class voters who expect more from a food bill. The red team has a similar broadening of its fan base to those concerned with government regulation, federal debt and "welfare" handouts—and their food policy goals seem to reflect all of this.

And Trump?

The most recent farm bill debate in 2018 was still the same ole, same ole. A Republican president calls for steep cuts to farm and nutrition programs, and Farm Bloc agriculture committee members from both parties circled the wagons to protect the farm bill—but for different reasons. Senate Agriculture Committee Chairman, Pat Roberts (Kansas), on the red team, declared his commitment to subsidized crop insurance: "We need to ensure that producers have risk management tools at their disposal." [30] Ranking member Debbie Stabenow (Michigan), on the blue team, focused on rural development and nutrition programs: "The Agriculture Department has made historic, targeted investments in rural communities to spur jobs and opportunity." She went on to criticize President Trump's budget for "gutting SNAP by nearly 30%."

As we noted in the introduction, politics is the allocation of values and resources. President Trump's budget promised to cut $231 billion from farm programs over several years. He has also reorganized the USDA to focus more on trade and less on rural development by elevating one and demoting the other. His secretary of agriculture, the former governor of Georgia, Sonny Perdue, seems poised to push for conservative roll backs of progressive programs while still trying to protect income programs for farmers. His first week in office he signed a directive to roll back stringent healthy school lunch requirements in the spirit of "making school meals great again."[31] These administrative values indicate a push toward red team austerity in agriculture and food programs, adding President Trump to our list of "villains", while a coalition of red and blue parochial farm bloc members tries held the line on the cuts. The 2018 Farm Bill ended up being almost a copy of 2014, and Congress merely named it the Agricultural Act of 2018, and act Trump signed since his tariff program against China had put farmgate prices much below expectations. President Trump did not issue any signing statements, but USDA Secretary Sonny Perdue commented in his USDA press release:

> This is a great day for our farmers, ranchers, foresters, and producers, as President Trump's signature on this bill is a Christmas present to

American agriculture. Farmers take financial risks every year as a matter of doing business, so having a Farm Bill in place gives them peace of mind to make their decisions for the future. Since early talks on this Farm Bill began back in 2017, I've always believed it would be more evolutionary, rather than revolutionary, and that has borne out to be true. The bill bolsters farm safety net programs, protects federal crop insurance, and maintains strong rural development and research initiatives. While we would have liked more progress on forest management reforms and work requirements for certain Supplemental Nutrition Assistance Program recipients, we look forward to using our authorities to make improvements in those areas. All told, this is a Farm Bill that should be welcomed by producers, and at USDA we will eagerly implement its provisions. At USDA, we were pleased to provide a tremendous amount of technical assistance to Congress as legislators wrote the bill. I thank the President for his leadership on this legislation, and commend the Senate and House Agriculture Committees for their many months of hard work.[32]

Here, again, we can see that USDA Secretaries can be very different from the President's they work for.

Far from Happily Ever After

The story of farming and food politics is not a fairytale, and political history in the real world does not end with the idea that the characters lived happily ever after. With self-interest and scarce political and economic resources at stake, competition should be expected. And that is exactly what our 100-year red-and-blue food fight has uncovered: cooperation is rare and even *it* is competitive.

So, where does the story leave our cast of characters? As promised, our story had revealed that farm and food support (and rural support and environmental support) is more at home with the Democratic Party than the Republican Party. Food policy is a legacy of New Deal interventionism, where the prevailing ethic expects and welcomes progressive government "smoothing" of the rough patches in rough and tumble capitalist practice. Democrats generally subscribe to this ethic, with a propensity to allow government and its budget to provide for the social welfare.[33] Opposing this view is the Republican faith in the free-market mechanisms to allocate scare resources efficiently, and the classically liberal (now conservative) conviction that freedom, individual initiative, private property, and personal (as opposed to state) responsibility are desirable over government direction of the economy and government (taxpayer) budgets to finance it. These are the ideological principles which guide the teams, and this has the very real effect of making the Red Team skeptical of federal farm and food programs, as we have seen.

Our story also revealed that farm and food support is more at home with Congress than with presidents, especially Republican presidents. Members of Congress serve at the pleasure of local districts and local desires. Red team and blue team members lost their jobs when they supported farm and food policy at odds with their voters. This makes members of Congress very attentive to parochial values. By contrast, presidents pursue a national agenda based on national, more ideological, values. Republican presidents particularly saw their role as one of pushing back on New Deal programs, including farm programs and nutrition assistance. This meant that almost every Republican president in the last 100 years has been notably hostile to conventional farm and food policy—and more recently to environmental and range-land conservation policy, when it comes at the expense of farmers and ranchers. As noted earlier, most farmers do not participate in USDA subsidy programs, but most farmers do have to deal with environmental regulation—making them potential supporters of red team Presidents.

Our story demonstrates conventional farm and food policy is more at home with the Farm Bloc than the rest of Congress. These are the core members of the Agricultural Committees in the House and Senate, and they tend to huddle together more often than they form opposing sides. It is this *handful* of players in red and blue jerseys that gives farm policy its "bipartisan" or nonpartisan reputation—and even *they* do not cooperate all the time on everything, as we have seen. Radical policies tend to open up the Farm Bloc to severe division, as with the 1949 Brennan Plan and the 1996 Freedom to Farm Plan.[34] Furthermore, the membership of these Agriculture Committees is evolving. In the old days, these members hailed from farm districts and farm states. In more recent times, urban and non-farm representatives have sought a place on the Agriculture Committee because the farm bill now covers more policies of interest to consumers and the poor,[35] pluralizing the meaning of food policy.

Finally, our story found that a surprising number of USDA secretaries are the enemies of business as usual in farm and food policy. Most recently, President Trump's appointment of Georgia Governor Sonny Perdue as Secretary of Agriculture resulted in an immediate reorganization of the USDA to satisfy red team goals, particularly the creation of an Undersecretary for Trade and the demotion of the rural development program. Other USDA Secretaries, in particular Ezra Taft Benson under President Eisenhower, are credited with increasing the partisanship of food policy. [36] In the most recent Biden administration, the re-appointment of Obama's USDA Secretary, Tom Vilsack after the 2020 election was viewed by many farm groups as a comforting move in an administration with more progressive appointments elsewhere.

At the root of this partisanship is the reality that the two teams have different goals, and that these goals are at opposite ends of the playing field. Hansen characterizes partisanship in farm and food policy as a party program which appeals to advocates, such as free-market supporters, with the obvious contrast, such as market intervention, appealing to the opposition party.[37] Smith and Seltzer emphasize the role of issues and policies, particularly the "ultimate issues" arising out of the New Deal (which divide liberals and conservatives) as the root cause of party polarization.[38] As our story has told us, Democrats and Republicans clearly pursue different farm and food policies *because* they are social welfare policies dependent on government expansion and taxpayer largess.

---

[1] Barnes, Bart. 1988. Barry Goldwater, GOP Hero, Dies. *The Washington Post* May 30, 1998.

[2] Eidenmuller, Michael E. 2008. Transcript of Ronald Reagan, A Time for Choosing delivered October 27th 1964. http://www.americanrhetoric.com/speeches/ronaldreaganatimeforchoosing.htm Last accessed October 20, 2016.

[3] Hansen p. 185.

[4] Ronald Reagan. 1981. Statement on Signing the Agriculture and Food Act of 1981. December 22, 1981 Reagan Library Archives.

[5] De Lama, George and Lea Donosky. 1985. "Regan Kills Farm Bill: No bailout for farmers in debt." Chicago Tribune March 7, 1985. http://articles.chicagotribune.com/1985-03-07/news/8501130185_1_veto-farm-programs-farmers (Last accessed November 30, 2016).

[6] DeLama

[7] Reagan Veto Speech 1985.

[8] Sheingate p. 201.

[9] Ronald Reagan's Food Security Act Signing Comments 1985.

[10] Ronald Reagan's Food Security Act Signing Comments 1985.

[11] Clift, Eleanor. 1985. Reagan Sign's History's Most Costly Farm Bill. LA Times. December 24, 1985. http://articles.latimes.com/1985-12-24/news/mn-20869_1_farm-bill (Last Accessed November 30, 2016.)

[12] Hansen p. 213

[13] Note 1962 Food and Drug Act, 1966 National Traffic and Motor Vehicle Safety Act, 1966 Fair Packaging and Labeling Act, 1968 Truth in Lending Act, 1972 Consumer Product Safety Act

[14] Hansen p. 190.

[15] Hansen p. 196

[16] Hansen p. 204

[17] Shiengate 2001, p. 197.

[18] Shiengate p. 201.

[19] Shiengate p. 201 at footnote 85.

[20] Shiengate p. 201.

[21] President Clinton Signing statement.

[22] Govtrack.com notes an incredible number of votes which were least predictable given the rest of the party's behavior in the chamber. Twenty Democratic Yea votes were statistically noteable: Alabama (2 districts), Florida (2 districts), Illinois (2 districts), Texas (4 districts) as well as single districts votes from Hawaii, Louisiana, Maryland, Mississippi, Missouri, New Jersey, New Mexico, Ohio, Virginia, and West Virginia. The 19 Republican Nay votes were concentrated in a handful of states: Florida (2 districts), Massachusetts (2 districts), New Jersey (6 districts), Wisconsin (5 districts) as well as single votes from Louisiana, Ohio, Tennessee, and Washington. (https://www.govtrack.ue/congress/104-1996/h42).

[23] Knutson, Ronald D. 2007. Agricultural and Food Policy (6th). Upper Saddle River NJ: Pearson Prentice Hall. p. 24

[24] Knutson p. 35

[25] Novak et al. p. 164

[26] See, for example, Daniel Imhoff. 2007. *Food Fight: The Citizen's Guide to the Next Food and Farm Bill*. Healdsburg, CA: Watershed Media.

[27] President George W. Bush. Veto Message on H.R. 2413. May 21, 2008.

[28] President George W. Bush. Veto Message on H.R. 2413. May 21, 2008.

[29] Remarks by the President at the Signing of the Farm Bill. February 7, 2014.

[30] Hagstrom, Jerry. 2017. "Senators: No Farm Bill Cuts." The Progressive Farmer. May 26, 2017.

[31] USDA. 2017. Ag Secretary Perdue Moves to Make School Meals Great Again. USDA Press release May 1, 2017.

[32] USDA. 2018. Statement of Secretary Perdue on President Trump's Signing of the Farm bill. USDA Press Release December 20, 2018.

[33] Scholars Smith and Seltzer note in their book (p. 4) that FDR "broke tradition" and "established a new orthodoxy in which the budget would be used as a tool to manage the economy" with the belief that a government grown economy could finance the growth in the welfare state. Financing the state required progressive income tax, an old guard Republican criticism. In explaining historic partisan polarization, Smith and Seltzer found (p. 5): "After the New Deal, the old guard in effect became a minority faction in the Republican Party as the ascendant moderates and liberals acquiesced to the New Deal notion of using income tax to finance the welfare state, and modestly redistribute income to maintain the basic features of a modern capitalistic economy. This acquiescence or accommodation of the Republican Party ended in 1964 when the old guard recaptured control of the Party and elected Reagan in 1980. Thereafter, the old-guard hostility to taxes and the welfare state became the new orthodoxy of the Republican Party and eventually a major source of polarization." See Robert C. Smith and Richard A. Seltzer. 2015. Polarization and the Presidency: From FDR to Barak Obama. Boulder, CO: Lynne Rienner Publishers.

[34] Sheingate, p. 202, notes 1996 Ag Committees felt they were "more divided than we've ever been."

[35] Hansen (p. 193) notes that Republican Peyser, a consumer advocate, sought a seat on the Agricultural Committee in 1974 and (p. 199) that urban Democrats ran for seats on the Ag subcommittee for food stamps in 1977.

[36] Hansen, p. 163, credits Ezra Taft Benson with "successful construction of farm policy as a partisan issue"

[37] Hansen, p. 163

[38] Smith and Seltzer, p. 2, noting that the material/ideological issues of taxes and social welfare are much more explanatory of enduring party polarization than the "social-moral issues" (abortion, gay rights) arising from the culture wars.

Chapter 6

Keeping Score: What Happens When an Expert Watches the Game

Now we arrive at the some of the academic meat in this book. The Heroes and Villains of the previous chapter showed us significant patterns in the way particular players and teams in certain eras approached food policy. A thoughtful foodie or farmer could not miss the central tendencies of partisans with regard to food and farming policy. This chapter purports to get more technical and look at the overall team stats with regard to food policy, particularly the level of competition and cooperation in congressional farm bills (1973-2018). In other words, we want to know just how cooperative or competitive is food policy? Is this a competitive issue? How competitive? If not, why not?

Our last chapter told an interesting story about food policy worth restating. *Food policy is about food votes*—votes from farmers and votes from consumers. More recently, farm policy is also about votes from citizens who are taxpayers, deficit hawks, environmentalists, and those concerned about poverty programs for nutrition and rural development. The preferences of these voters motivated many of the heroes and villains of the last chapter, especially members of Congress. On the other hand, food policy is also about principles, about ideas of the good society and what good government looks like. Should government intervene in the food economy? If so, how much, and, in what way? These are the questions in the minds of politicians, and the last chapter noted the heroes and villains, especially presidents, were often motivated by principles. In terms of the farmer and foodie vote, we learned that the congressional Farm Bloc and, to some extent, the Democratic Party itself generally supported farm and food social welfare programming. We also learned that Republican presidents are much more likely to oppose business as usual with regard to farm and table subsidies.

But what about *team* play in the modern food policy era? Politicians make their most important plays by voting too—they vote as Members of the House, as Senators or as Presidents to support or oppose policy. Do the red and blue teams line up on different sides of the field, or do they all stand together and advance the policy down the field unopposed? When there is opposition, who is on the other side and what colors are they wearing? Is offense and defense really red-and-blue or is it some blend of part-red, part-blue on each side? In other words, do Republicans and Democrats cooperate or compete when it comes to food policy? Are their agendas really that different or is it "Twiddledum and Twiddledee"—as some have suggested?[1] To get to the bottom of our question, we need to compare team play, and find out what are the team voting patterns on modern food bills. In this spirit, we will take the time to examine the official line ups for food and farm policy.

Making the question more interesting is the modern practice of bundling separate programs and policies together into "omnibus" or catch-all farm bills. As noted in the introduction, American farm bills pursue many values all related to food and fiber provision in the U.S.: commodities, conservation, trade, nutrition, credit, rural development, research, forestry, energy, horticulture, crop insurance, disadvantaged farmers, etc. Are contemporary food bills so omnibus (catch-all) in nature, that there is literally something for everyone, making opposition rare? Might this mean something-for-everyone approach mean no one ever really votes against it? But—what if someone still does? What exactly are they opposing, and why? If politicians or whole teams do oppose the bill, it wouldn't it be even more proof of a lack of cooperation in food policy when even a catch-all bill could not obtain their support? This is what makes an analysis of team play so interesting— we can see *who* supported *what* and *why*.

The Puzzle of Partisanship in Food Policy: What Happens When Scholars Watch the Game

Before we analyze the teams, we need to understand debate. When you invite a scholar to watch the game, you will inevitably end up with a debate. This research is motivated by an academic puzzle in food and agriculture policy. According to scholars and policymakers, food and agriculture policy is overwhelmingly considered bipartisan due to its locally-focused, log-rolling and "distributive" nature.[2] In terms of localism, agriculture interests were historically widely dispersed across the majority of geographically based House districts. This meant that farm interests were often local interests. As late as 1950, two-thirds of American counties were "farming dependent"[3] having at least 15% of residents' earnings or employment arising from the agricultural sector. This meant that farm interests translated into voter interests for most House districts.

In terms of "logrolling", agriculture policy was the poster-child exemplar of members without anything in common trading votes—especially the huge "logroll" incorporating the Food Stamp program (a poverty program disproportionately benefiting urban districts) into the Farm Bill, which was mostly an agriculture and rural development bill.[4] In terms of "distributive" politics, distributive programs are programs which take *general* revenue and give it to specific clientle. These programs tend to have *broad* costs (to all taxpayers, especially urban taxpayers) and *concentrated* benefits (to farmers, the poor, and rural communities). These programs also usually pass by consensus,[5] garnering the support of most every member of Congress, because they have a large benefit for constituents and a relatively modest individual cost to taxpayers.[6] Scholars of farm policy have found evidence of this kind of bipartisan, "distributive" voting.[7] It is fun to pass out the money and bring home the bacon.

For farm commodity programs, partisanship fights over the details of the goodie bag gave way to bipartisan cooperation on different goodie bags for different farmers. Sheingate (2001) notes that parties used to exploit win-lose policies among producers of different commodities to capture votes for *their* team, such as the appeal to corn growers at the expense of cotton or tobacco. Under the old system all farmers had to live under one policy, but which *one* meant some farmers won while others lost (such as the reduction of parity payments in return for more planting freedom—something benefiting corn growers, but devastating to cotton and tobacco farmers). However, after 1965, that source of one-size-not-fitting-all conflict largely went away (though President Trump's 2018 program to "bail out" soybean farmers brought protests from corn farmers and other food producers with reduced profit margins under trade tariff policies). The creation of *individual* commodity programs with individually tailored subsidy packages for each crop (one for wheat, one for cotton, one for sugar, one for dairy) and individual commodity lobby groups (who could work with either party, depending on geography or requests for more or less government help and oversight of their industry) created incentives to cooperate on farm policy. Scholars attribute such voluntary and individualized commodity programs with finding bi-partisanship among members of Congress from 1960 to 1980, with less than one-third of roll call votes on agriculture were partisan during this period.[8] For this part of the debate, even recent scholars still refer to agriculture as the "quieter milieu" in terms of partisan conflict.[9]

That said, there is also a flurry of recent food policy books which squarely places food and agricultural policy in partisan terms. Daniel Imhoff's farm bill treatise for the common citizen *Food Fight: The Citizen's Guide to the Next Farm Bill,*[10] walks a voter through the farm bill title-by-title with illustrations of ideological winners and losers in farm policy, complete with a forward by liberal food policy critic Michael Pollan. Similarly, Marion Nestle's well-researched *Food Politics: How the Food Industry influences Nutrition and Health,*[11] also warned of industry-serving federal policy run amok. A third book, Jayson Lusk's

Food Police: A Well-fed Manifesto About the Politics of Your Plate,[12] likewise illuminates the progressive politics (and conservative criticisms) inherent in current food policy. Three of these books portrayed food politics in ideological terms, the first two notably liberal in their critique of distributive corporate programs, and the latter notably conservative in defense of capitalism, efficiency and modern food production. This seems to indicate something is afoot in agriculture policy with regard to partisanship and politics, something political scientist, Christopher Bosso, asserts in *Framing the Farm Bill: Interests, Ideology and the Agricultural Act of 2014.*[13]

Indeed, there is some scholarly support for a *partisan* view of agriculture policy. First, there is the history of partisan proclivities more known to agriculture policy wonks and economists than to politics scholars.[14] As explained in Chapter Four, federal food policy started with the liberal progressives of the early 1900's pursuing food safety and with New Deal Liberal Agriculture policy in the 1930's. Since this era there is a long history of Democratic Party support for fixed supports in agriculture, even under the Truman and Kennedy Administrations. By contrast, there is a history of free-market or at least flexible price supports pursued by Eisenhower, a Republican. While the early parties clearly took positions, and constituent farm groups such as the NFU (Democrat) and the AFB (Republican) took partisan sides, the geography of crop production did not perfectly match political party control, and Southern Democrats would routinely side with Republicans against production controls, based on the commodities grown in the South. Thus, there is the appearance of bipartisanship, but in reality, stakeholders understood where the political parties stood on agricultural support issues.

Even in recent times, notable partisan votes have occurred. In the beginning of the modern era, 1965, only 19 Republicans (farm state members) voted with Democrats to pass the farm bill.[15] Similarly, Congressional scholars Hurwitz, Moiles, and Rhode noted a series of *partisan* House votes for agriculture in the 104th Congress (1994-1996).[16]

Second, there is the very real fact that federal food and agriculture policy was not immune to the pressures of a period of liberal mobilization in the early 1970's.[17] This mobilization saw the formation of the EPA, OSHA, and CPSC, and the incorporation of the Food Stamp poverty program into the Farm Bill first occurred in 1973, showing some non-farm "liberal" values encroachment into traditional food and agriculture policy. Thus, we are left with a puzzle: *just how partisan is food and agriculture policy?* Do Democrats and Republicans play together on this issue, or are the teams competing for different food and farming goals?

Why Partisanship? Why Now?

Fewer Farmers Feeding More Voters

In general, there are reasons to believe conventional notions of "bi-partisan" farm policy might be changing. First, there is the fact that America is not a nation of farmers anymore. As noted above, two-thirds of U.S. Counties (and by extension a significant portion of House Districts) were historically farm-dependent. In 2010, that figure dropped to less than one-sixth.[18] This means there are a lot fewer Members of Congress who hail from "farm country." It is even worse for "farm states" most of which have diversified their economies beyond farming. As noted by Mercier, even states with significant farming activities may only have a mere handful of House districts that are actually farming dependent. This means even states with large farm production numbers like Illinois and California are driven by issues other than farming. In the U.S. overall, only about two million farmers exist—a fraction of votes in a nation with 330 million people. Not only is the farm huddle smaller, but it has made supporting farm plays and farm goals much less important in the day-to-day work of "farm" players in government, reducing the need for commodity program supporters to work with supporters of other areas of agricultural policy.[19] This has made players in the farm huddle less dependent on each other and thus, less willing to stick together as a team of its own. This reality is demonstrated in the uneasy confidence of 2018 House and Senate Agriculture Committee members trying to present a united front even as they leaked information about difficult disagreements. "Predictability and stability is what we need", said Republican Agriculture Committee Chair Pat Roberts (Kansas) of 2018 farm bill negotiations while Democrat House Agriculture Committee Chair Collin Peterson (Minnesota) claimed "we never should have written a farm bill [in 2014] now this is what we have to deal with."[20] The members were also protecting their geographic interests because 2014 policy had benefited Kansas wheat farmers more than Minnesota dairy and sugar beet growers.

Parties that are "Poles" Apart

Second, there is the rise of polarization among so-called red and blue voters[21] and the ideological conservative and liberal sorting of parties, where moderates of either party tend to be rarer. These periods of party polarization and divided government can disrupt normally cooperative congressional agreements. Farm bloc members have notoriously used nutrition poverty programs to attract urban members to support rural needs. However, in particularly partisan years (such as the farm bill votes of 1996, 2014, 2018) members are much less willing to cooperate with party members on the other side. Divided government (where one party controls the presidency and the other controls Congress) can also signal strong, competitive parties, where each side is more confident in pursuit of its separate goals.

This polarization and ideological sorting begun in the 1970's has reached near purity in recent congressional policymaking. Indeed, CQ Researcher famously noted that 2009 "was the most partisan year ever,"[22] and commentators lament the loss of "moderates" such as Republican Senator Richard Lugar (Indiana) in agriculture policy. [23] The 2014 Farm Bill saw the *historic* separation of the nutrition title (which includes SNAP and school lunch) form the rest of the farm bill, a tactic widely perceived as the death knell for rural-urban (Red and Blue) cooperation on farm and food policy.[24] This final iteration of farm bill partisan politics is widely compared to 1996 because both years saw strong emphasis on fiscal conservatism from Republican "ideologues"—effectively ending compromises and business as usual for federal farm and food programs.[25] Similar to the way parity tinkering opened up farm policy to party fights; recent tinkering in the SNAP program destabilized the usual votes. President Trump's USDA secretary, similar to secretaries of old, proposed scrapping SNAP in favor of pre-packaged boxes of food—an idea gaining little traction, but certainly continuing the not-so-usual proclivities of the USDA to challenge conventional policy approaches to food and farming.

A "Farm" Bill in Name Only

Third, there is the growth of the farm bill itself, to incorporate numerous issues appealing to Democrats and Republicans. Farm Bills have a "something for everyone" approach that crosses party lines, as exhibited in poverty, environmental, trade and rural development programs. However, current parties are showing enduring signs of parting ways. Scholars and journalists agree that the House decision to separate the 2014 Farm Bill vote from the SNAP vote was a historic break.[26] Republicans limited farm spending and food stamp spending for reasons of fiscal and budget concern. Democrats pushed a food policy that is heavy on government social goals: health, poverty and the environment. Both parties still supported liberalized trade policies. Scholars define a *partisan* issue as one which invokes the interests of *competing* partisan electoral coalitions,[27] and a closer look at federal farm policy and political party platforms shows signs of renewed partisan and ideological splintering on food and agriculture policy.

Different Farms, Different Food, Different Politics

Fourth, farming and food production is not a monolithic, unified industry or political interest group. Rather it has a host of historic and current diversification, providing opportunities for parties to represent some farmers at the expense of others. As noted above, some commodity coalitions separated from historic party-geography support (e.g., Democrats and Southern Cotton growers) when commodity programs became "stand alone" programs for each crop after 1965. This subdivision of farmers enabled growers to work with either party in order to secure preferential treatment. Beyond commodities, the farm bill now supports horticulture, organic certification and livestock production. These interests are often at odds with commodity growers. For instance, livestock and milk producers prefer cheap, abundant grain. Organic growers prefer a level playing field with conventional growers. Small farmers ask for exemptions to compete with large-scale producers. This more modern diversification of federal farm programs (organic provisions were added in 2002, with small-farm USDA exceptions in 2014, permanent disaster relief for livestock producers was added in 2014) may also find more partisan homes. To the extent that organic production is associated with environmentally friendly food production (Democratic issue ownership), or to the extent that livestock production is associated with grazing of public lands (Republican issue ownership), the issue has the potential for partisan divide. Indeed many of the goals of stakeholders in the farm bill are in regular conflict, especially as the group of beneficiaries has grown. [28] To the extent these diversified constituencies typically align with either party, partisan agricultural policy may evolve.

The "Moral" Side of Food Production

Fifth, food and agriculture production is leaving its traditional fold of narrow economic, material concerns and exhibiting elements of broader moral concerns, opening it up to more ideology and less compromise. People can compromise on economic goals, such negotiating how much to cut or grow a program. People have a harder time supporting programs that conflict with their beliefs about the good life. Commodity programs, regardless of costs, may seem "immoral" to someone concerned about industrial, grain-dependent agriculture. Fruit and vegetable-only promotion may not make sense to someone who feels meat and dairy offer nutrient-dense foods or that grains keep storable calories in reach for the poor. Grass-fed beef may seem like a waste of resources per-pound of protein, or appear to be a sustainable livestock program, depending on your values.

According to scholars, morality policy concerns debates about "first principles" and values, rather than the choice of a policy instrument. [29] Newer food and agriculture production and consumption values, such as animal rights, organic and environmental purity, local food movements, the use of biotechnology and GMOs, and school nutrition programs, have taken on moral overtones approaching absolutes about the morally correct way to produce or consume food. [30] As noted by Wilson (2006), compromise on these "post-material" issues is problematic since it requires compromise on values and beliefs. Historically, food and agriculture policy was about material concerns such as production, economy and safety [31] and the main arguments were about *instruments* to obtain those goals. These newer issues change the *goals* themselves, sparking radical disagreement. [32]

To the extent political parties, and the people who support them, align with these moral feelings, food and agriculture policy may find ideological, partisan homes. As noted above, scholars define a *partisan* issue as sparks competition and lines teams up on opposite sides of issues.[33]

Foodies and Farmers in the Stands

Sixth, the party in the electorate—the fan base—is exhibiting both partisan and bipartisan behavior when it comes to food and agriculture policy. In terms of current partisanship among farmers, Sheingate (2001) notes that farmers historically voted about equally Democrat and Republican, with Democrats enjoying a very slight edge from 1972-1992. However, voting among farmers has become much more partisan in recent elections. In 2012, Pulse Opinion Research reported 51% of farmers identified Republican while only a 26% identified Democrat in a survey of large commercial farmers (550 acres or more).[34] That same election the Farm Journal reported 85% of rural respondents in an on-line poll voting for Romney over Obama.[35] Journalists also noted the rural/urban divide in voter turnout in 2012, noting urban areas become 32% more Democratic while rural areas become 11% more Republican,[36] and that Romney (Republican) won 61% of the rural vote. For 2016, the disparities were even starker as 67% of farmers said they voted for Trump (versus 24% for Clinton).[37] These numbers might suppose greater Republican (partisan) support for those parts of food and agriculture policy that are farm focused or rural in nature.

However, while farmers and rural voters are becoming more partisan, public opinion about agriculture subsidies is still quite bi-partisan. Many polls show little partisan difference in support for farm subsidies. A 2009 World Public Opinion (from the Program on International Policy Attitudes at the University of Maryland) reports only 36% of Republicans and 35% of Democrats favor "US Government subsidies for large farming businesses." The same poll also reports 77% of Republican respondents and 83% of Democratic respondents support US government subsidies for "small farmers who farm less than 500 acres."[38] Likewise a 2011 Gallup poll showed similar partisan attitudes toward programs with 42% of Republicans and 48% of Democrats favoring a cut in spending for "Farm aid".[39] A 2018 poll from Politico and the Harvard T.H. Chan School of Public Health also reported continued even support for increasing farm subsidies to small and medium-size operations (44% Republicans, 47% Democrats, and 46% Independents).[40] Thus, even for the fans, the question remains, just how partisan is food and agriculture policy?

Modern Food Policy: A Brief History of Famous Farm Bills

Contemporary food policy is largely written into catch-all farm bills. These bills have a chapter for almost every food provision and farm related value in America.

As noted in the introduction to this book, the most recent farm bill (2014) had twelve titles covering topics like commodities, rural development, nutrition, conservation and so on. (*See Table 1, page 2.*) Most scholars agree that 1973 was the first modern farm bill. It was the first to contain a Nutrition title and permanent nation-wide food stamp programming. Just like you would not compare modern sports to players and teams in the 1930's and 1940's, you cannot compare policy votes in 1940 to policy votes in 1980—the policy just wasn't the same. For this reason comparing Red and Blue votes only on these modern farm bills is a fairly uniform measure of partisan competition in food policy.

Table 4. List of U.S. Congressional Farm Bills 1973-2018

Agricultural Improvement Act of 2018 (2018)
Agricultural Act of 2014 (2014)
Food and Energy Security Act (2008)
Farm Security and Rural Investment Act (2002)
Federal Agricultural Improvement and Reform Act (FAIR) (1996) a.k.a "Freedom to Farm"
Food Agriculture Conservation and Trade Act (1990)
Food Security Act (1985)
Agriculture and Food Act (1981)
Food and Agriculture Act (1977)
Agriculture and Consumer Protection Act (1973)

Table 4 lists the farm bills passed since 1973. These bills have special reputations among the policy experts (largely agricultural economists) who study them, and it makes sense for us to hit the highlights of each year. This will provide some context for the team line-ups we explore later in the chapter.

Big Money for Nutrition Programs

First, there is the beginning of big money for nutrition programs. The *Agricultural and Consumer Protection Act of 1973* is famous for adding the Nutrition title to make the Food Stamp Program a permanent part of the farm bill and the USDA budget. While small at first, nutrition spending ($12.2 billion) eclipsed commodity spending ($10 billion) in the 1985 farm bill. By the time of the 2014 farm bill, nutrition assistance (including WIC, TEFAP and school lunch) was 80% ($391 billion over five years) and commodity spending was 13% (24 billion over five years). Thus, all parties recognize that nutrition spending is the *biggest* part of national food and farm policy. Nutrition spending has also been a way for rural districts and farmers to obtain support from urban districts and consumers. In terms of lobbyists, nutrition spending unites farmers, food processors and grocers—all of which benefit from more food dollars in the hands of consumers.

The marriage of poverty policy and farm policy has been an important union for obtaining mutual support from both sets of supporters, and this partially explains why blue players vote for a farm subsidy and red players vote for a nutrition subsidy.

Freedom for Farmers

Second, there is the conservative "freeing" of farmers and government from farm subsidy programs and the simultaneous "volunteering" of ag to take more responsibility for environmental conservation, which is what happened in the *1996 Freedom to Farm* policy. This bill took a decidedly conservative turn under a Republican House conservative push back on liberal spending programs. This is the same Congress that revamped cash welfare with work requirements and five-year benefit limits. In the same spirit, the farm reform act of 1996 removed production controls and significantly reduced subsidies to farmers under a free-market "freedom to farm" distribution policy that no longer tied commodity payment to planting decisions. Farmers were "free" plant what they wanted, as much as they wanted, and receive shrinking subsidy payment, supposedly reduced to zero over time, thus eventually "freeing" government from the business of supporting farming. The goal of the 1996 farm bill was to wean the agricultural economy away from farm subsidies over about seven years.

At the same time, the 1996 farm bill also added the Conservation title and voluntary conservation programs to incorporate new issues important to contemporary voters. Voluntary programs give farmers extra benefits for making environmentally friendly changes to their farm. Some programs rewarded habitat set-asides by "renting" the un-farmed ground from the farmer. Other programs offered to pay a portion of the costs to upgrade facilities to protect water or soil, especially big facilities, like feedlots. While many citizens may be surprised a conservative Congress assented to broad new environmental programs for agriculture, the programs were largely voluntary cost-share programs designed to be win-win for farmers and the environment. It was also a way to avoid more heavy-handed regulation by the Environmental Protection Agency, since farm conservation programs are administered by the local farm friendly Soil Conservation or Natural Resources office. Since the 1996 farm bill is a conservative reform bill, we might expect it to stand out in terms of team play and team dynamics, with a higher amount of support from the Red team.

Bringing More Farmers to the Table

Later bills simply kept expanding programs. The *2002* farm bill restored more generous farm subsidies cut back in 1996 because of a commodity market down turn, and added new provisions for livestock and specialty crops (fruits and vegetables)—products which had not received permanent federal help in the past. The 2002 farm bill also added national program to certify organic farm products.

The *2008* farm bill contained an energy title and energy conservation benefits. In a post 9-11 world, the 2008 farm bill sought to help reduce dependence on foreign fuels by promoting alternative fuels from corn and biomass. As social welfare bills go, this gave conservative politicians concerned about national security a reason to support the farm bill. It was also touted as a pro-environment move to wean the nation from fossil fuels. The 2008 farm bill also changed the food stamp program to the Supplemental Nutrition Assistance Program, now giving eligible households electronic SNAP food dollars instead of paper food stamps.

Too Big to Fail?

By *2014*, the catch-all farm bill is going to have so many balls in the air, politicians of all stripes will begin to question its wisdom. Conservatives trying to reign in federal spending are going wanted both farmers and the poor to reduce their dependence on the federal coffers, especially because of ballooning payments to corporate farms and expanding enrollments in SNAP programs. To kill farm subsidies and nutrition program growth, these politicians moved to divorce the farm bill from the nutrition title. Their hope was that many blue team players would not vote for a farm bill which heavily subsidized corporate farms, and that red team players would vote to drastically reduce nutrition program spending—which had now become eighty percent of the farm bill. As noted earlier, cooperation between more moderate players, especially in the Senate, kept most of the farm and nutrition programs from relatively intact. However, the possibility of breaking up the farm bill into separate votes has made the farm bill vulnerable to partisan bickering in a manner similar to the rigid or flexible price support wars of earlier eras.

Knowing a little about the reputations and realities of these farm bills sets the stage for considering team support for farm policy. But we also need to remind ourselves of the political context itself.

Modern Food Politics: An Insider's Guide to the Game

While special interests fight for every "jot and tittle" of every chapter, and members of Congress will often go to bat for particular provisions near and dear to them, their fans or their sponsors, at the end of the day the bill passes or fails with a vote. Or, actually, several votes—one from the House, one from the Senate and a veto or signature of the President. By looking at the team stats for these votes, we can measure the degree of partisanship (team competition) in food policy.

So which votes should we look at? In order to compare apples to apples (or perhaps corn to corn!), we should start with the contemporary partisan era, which most scholars fix as post-1968. This period formed fairly stable party coalitions, where fairly predictable fans and issues support the red and blue teams. As noted in Chapter Two, the red team tends to dominate rural and heartland areas, and their coalition includes corporate free-market interests, guns rights and religious conservatives. The blue team tends to dominate the Northeast and West Coast and Urban areas, including small manufacturing or university towns. Their coalition includes labor, minorities and environmentalists. Both teams are also fairly consistent in their support or opposition for extending New Deal social welfare and corporate regulatory programs. Scholars also tend to agree that the parties began to significantly polarize after 1968, steadily losing moderate members in favor of more liberal or more conservative members with each election cycle. Today the parties are considered "poles apart" on most issues, with little common ground. With this in mind, Farm Bills from 1973-2018 have been chosen as the modern era of partisan teams, and era which nicely coincides with the modern content of the bills themselves.

Technical Partisanship

Just how partisan were these bills? Political scientists define a partisan bill as one where a majority of one party votes against the majority of the other party.[41] Bills where this occurs can be labeled "partisan" and the resulting bill referred to as the Republican Farm Bill or the Democratic Farm Bill. Bills where a *majority* of both parties support the bill can truly be called *bi*partisan. Politicians define partisanship differently. If a handful of members of the other team support a bill, politicians will claim bipartisan support for their bill, including presidents. Since we are interested in team play, we will look at the team stats in the scientific rather than political sense—and only recognize a bill as bipartisan when a majority of both parties support it. The willingness of most members of a team to move the ball down the field signals party positions on the issues much more than the movements of a few rogue players.

Not One Vote, but Four!

Nothing is simple in policymaking, and passing a farm bill requires more than one vote in Congress. After drafting the bill and marking it up in various committees, success will culminate in bringing the bill to a vote in the chamber (House or Senate). This gives the teams the opportunity to show their true colors. Are they united or are they opposed? Farm Bills typically have *four* votes. To appreciate the game, we have to appreciate the rules, so indulge me a minute while I explain why a farm bill requires four votes instead of just one. The Constitution requires the House and Senate to pass the *same exact* bill. However, much of the time the chambers will pass their own version of the bill—a House version and a Senate version. These two separate bills have to be re-crafted into a single bill, sent back to the chambers, and voted on again. This recrafting is usually negotiated in a "conference committee" with representatives from both the House and the Senate hashing out their differences and trading more concessions to reach a deal. The resulting compromise, a Conference bill, is then sent to each chamber for a formal vote. Thus, farm bills have four votes, one to pass the House bill, one to pass the Senate bill, and House and Senate votes on the Conference Bill.

The House vs. the Senate

As noted in the Introduction to this book, House bills tend to be more extreme than Senate bills because House members are elected every two years, represent smaller often more homogeneous districts, and are more subject to turnover. The House is also more top-down in its procedures, making House bills more of a party-line type bill, driven by the party leaders of the chamber. Senators, on the other hand, are more independent and more inclined to moderation in policy development as a rule, due to chamber norms and requirements forcing compromise. For this reason, we might expect more partisanship in the House than in the Senate. We would also expect conference bills to be more moderate than House bills and closer to Senate bills, as was the case in 2014 discussed in the introduction. House and Senate bills are never the same, so the chambers form a conference committee to reconcile the differences and present the new "reconciled" bill back to each chamber. Conference Bills typically receive more votes from both teams, as a rule, since members are more vested in the bill and the process itself. Is it is also often the case that offending parts of bills have been cut out or significantly modified in conference, so that members who voted *against* are now more comfortable voting *for*.

The rest of this chapter offers team stats and numbers for the reader who gets into data.

Farm Teams

The first way to look for partisanship is to simply compare how many farm bill votes were partisan. With ten farm bills and about four votes per bill, this gives us roughly 40 votes to look at. We can then count the number of bills supported only by a majority of Democrats, only by a majority of Republicans or supported by a majority of both teams. Table 5 lists the votes according to majority team support. Counting the votes this way, eight were Republican, nine were Democratic and eighteen were bipartisan. This means the parties are on opposite sides of food policy about *half* the time. With numbers like this, it appears political scientists can have it both ways. I can argue that food policy is partisan, and my colleagues can argue that it is bipartisan. It depends on if you think disagreeing half the time is a high or low amount. For my part, I can also argue that farm policy is just as likely to be partisan as not, making claims of bipartisanship far from the norm.

We might expect that all of the partisan votes were for a House or a Senate Bill, with conference bills—the one's that count—being bipartisan. However, Table 5 reveals a different story. Five of the Republican support bills and four of the Democratic support bills were votes on conference votes. This means that the compromise farm policy in conference votes is still quite partisan, with only one team significantly moving the ball down the field.

Also of interest is the timing and severity of partisanship—does it seem to be getting worse or better? As Table 5 demonstrates partisan votes were just as likely before 1996 as after, with nine votes occurring before and nine votes occurring after. On the bipartisan side, the cooperation is slightly more likely before 1996, with eleven bipartisan votes occurring before and ten votes occurring after. However, things are still roughly even at this vantage point. By comparing these votes, there is not much evidence that partisanship is increasing or decreasing. It stays about the same. As the last chapter on the bipartisan history of food policy demonstrated, partisanship is as old as farm programs themselves. There were no good old days of perfect cooperation. Food policy has had its share of partisan competition across the years, even with modern farm bills.

Like any sport, we expect the hometown team to have an advantage, and Congress is no different. The party in charge of the chamber tends to have its way and push its agenda at the expense of the other team. Partisan votes tend to reflect the majority leadership of the chamber, but not perfectly so. In 1981, the minority party (Republicans) joined with a minority of Democrats to secure passage of a House Conference vote. In terms of democracy, this is good news. If foodies and farmers vote a party into Congress, that party stands a good chance of writing a partisan farm bill and obtaining party support.

Table 5. Partisan Support for Farm Bills

Republican Support (% of R voting Yea--% of D voting Yea)
2018 House Floor* (92-0)
2014 House Floor* (95-0), House Conference* (72-43)
1996 House Floor* (91-28), Senate Conference* (98-46)
1985 Senate Conference* (68-48)
1981 House Conference (67-35), Senate Floor* (84-31), Senate Conference* (84-50)

TOTAL 9 votes (22%)

Democratic Support (% of D voting Yea--% of R voting Yea)
2014 Senate Conference* (83-48)
2008 House Floor* (93-9)
2002 Senate Floor* (96-19), Senate Conference* (86-41)
1981 House Floor* (75-29)
1977 House Floor* (83-49), House Conference* (85-47)
1973 House Floor* (61-47), House Conference* (88-29)

TOTAL 9 votes (22%)

Bi-partisan Support (majority of both parties)
2018 House Conference (98D-80R) Senate Floor (100D-77R) Senate conference (100D-74R)
2014 Senate Floor (UC)
2008 House Conference (94D-51R), Senate Floor (93D-77R), Senate Conference (97D-76R)
2002 House Floor (72R-69D), House Conference (66D-65R)
1996 House Conference (92R-59D)
1990 House Floor (UC), House Conference (80D-70R), Senate Floor (80R-74D), Senate Conference (69R-57D)
1985 House Floor (74D-55R), House Conference (79D-73R), Senate Floor (69R-67D)
1977 Senate Floor (88D-65R), Senate Conference (91D-87R)
1973 Senate Floor (95D-80R), Senate Conference (98D-87R)

TOTAL 21 votes (52%)

Unknown
1996 Senate Floor (voice vote)

*Party controls the chamber (1981 House Conference only exception)

The Real Difference is Conference Play

The story of team stats is not yet finished. When it comes to food policy, citizens really only care about policies that become actual laws. The scrimmages of chamber floor votes mean nothing when the real bill is the conference bill. This is the bill the President will sign. This is the bill that will become the law of the land. Everyone knows it. And everyone knows that chamber versions are really just bluffs to set the stage for negotiation. Republican chambers will pass really *red* bills. Democratic chambers will pass really *blue* bills.[42] House bills will be more extreme than Senate bills. However, of the seventeen partisan farm bill votes, half of those were a conference vote. Likewise, of the eighteen bipartisan farm bill votes, half of those were for a House or Senate version of the bill. Again, there is no sense that partisanship is reserved only for extreme chamber bills. That said, most (70%) House Floor farm bill votes were partisan while most (75%) Senate Floor farm bill votes were bipartisan.

But what about overall team voting for farm bills. If everyone is voting for a conference bills, regardless if they are a House member or a Senate member, why not just look at party voting for conference bills. We will just put all House players and Senate players on the field at the same time with the same ball (the Conference Bill) and see which jerseys run which way. This is where the bipartisan camp may have the advantage.

Table 6 examines only conference votes, for it is here that all parties in all chambers are voting on the exact *same* policy. This chart lumps all the team mates together, regardless of chamber. Thus a truer test of partisan difference can be found in a comparison of roll-call votes on Conference bills. In other words, we compare the percentage of red players supporting a bill to the percentage of blue players supporting a bill and come up with some interesting observations.

First, notice most of the time most players regardless of their jersey vote yes on Conference bills. We can also look at average team support for farm bills. As Table 6 illustrates, parties supported farm bill conference votes at the exact same level (68%) on average from 1973-2018. Similarly, all but the 1981 farm bill conference vote qualifies as 'bi-partisan,' meaning a majority members from both parties supported the bill. Admittedly, conference votes may be a blunt measure of party support. Haskell (2010) maintains that members of Congress have an incentive to see a bill pass once it has reached the conference stage, leading to larger margins of support than House and Senate version votes. Thus, in terms of the number of red jerseys and blue jerseys voting yes, both teams seem to be actively moving the ball down the field in the same direction. However, a comparison of Table 5 and Table 6 shows eight *conference* votes with only Republican or Democratic support. How can it be both ways? Well Table 6 is simply counting bodies, but those bodies may be concentrated on J.V. (House) or on Varsity (Senate). At a Varsity game (conference vote) only red or blue—but not both—will be moving the ball in a single direction. Take another look at table

5 and you will notice those partisan conference votes in each chamber are pretty lopsided: 1973 House Conference (88D -29R) or 1996 Senate Conference (98R – 46 D), for instance.

Scholars also expect the House to be more partisan and the Senate to be more collegial,[43] and more bi-partisan in its final votes. Indeed, much of Senate business is conducted through negotiated Unanimous Consent agreements or simple unanimous consent votes. Table 7 allows us to look down each column to see if partisanship is just a House problem or if it surfaces in the Senate, too. Here, the House was indeed more partisan on floor votes on House version bills (6 out of 9 votes) than the Senate (2 out of nine votes, counting the 1996 voice vote as bipartisan). However, with conference votes, the House reverses course and becomes much more bi-partisan (5 out nine), even surpassing the Senate (4 out of nine) in this data. Thus, team stats are not completely the result of chamber practices.

One other interesting fact arises from this analysis of conference votes. As we said above, this is the vote that counts, the vote that will mean there *is* a farm bill. Do the parties tend to support farm bills evenly? Or is one set of jerseys more likely to vote yes when the rubber hits the road? As Table 6 shows, parties are still widely variable in their support. Most of the bills showed a significant difference in the percentage of red and blue jerseys supporting the bill. Most conference bills had widely lopsided support, in spite of the overall 66% average for each team. The 2008 farm bill garnered 94% of the Democratic vote and only 55% of the Republican vote. The 1996 farm bill obtained 93% of the Republican vote and only 56% of the Democratic vote. While technically most votes are considered bipartisan because a majority of both voted *Yea*, significant party differences, even in conference votes, are the norm. This implies that foodies, farmers and all citizens have a menu of choices when it comes to the food politics they are served. If they order the Red Daily Deal or the Blue Plate Special, chances are that it will not be the same *My Plate* brought to the table.

Stepping back to examine roll-call data, there is no clear pattern of increasing partisanship overtime, across chambers or with-in chambers. Rather, according to the stats, it appears that modern farm policy is still a somewhat bi-partisan effort.[44] Farm policy is bi-partisan about half the time and partisan about half the time, with minorities of *each* party skeptical of current food and agriculture policy according to their (separate) norms. Keeping the farm bill "omnibus" has often contained many of these potential fracture lines in food and agriculture policy. However, if the farm bill no longer catches *all* food values, as we saw with the Republican attempt to remove nutrition values from the farm bill in 2014, partisanship is a proven reality in food policy, always on the sidelines waiting for a substitution and a game-winning play to steal the lead.

Table 6. Partisan Support by Conference Vote Across the House & Senate

PERCENT OF PARTY VOTING YEA ON CONFERENCE VOTE

	Republicans	Democrats	Percentage Difference		Bipartisan or Partisan?
2018	85%	98%	13%	D	BI
2014	67	50	17	R	BI
2008	55	94	39	D	BI
2002	61	70	9	D	BI
1996	93	56	37	R	BI
1990	69	75	6	D	BI
1985	72	75	3	D	BI
1981	71	38	33	R	R
1977	53	86	33	D	BI
1973	57	56	1	R	BI
Mean	68%	68%	19%	D	BI

Partisan votes (D or R) indicate a majority of one party voted in support against a majority of the other party.
Bipartisan votes (BI) indicate a majority of both parties supported the conference bill.

Table 7. Farm Bill Partisanship by Chamber Support

	H Floor	S Floor	H Conference	S Conference
2018	R	BI	BI	BI
2014	R	BI	R	D
2008	D	BI	BI	BI
2002	BI	D	BI	D
1996	R	(voice vote)	BI	R
1990	BI	BI	BI	BI
1985	BI	BI	BI	R
1981	D	R	R	R
1977	D	BI	D	BI
1973	D	BI	D	BI
Total D	4	1	2	2

Total Democratic 9 votes

| Total R | 3 | 1 | 2 | 3 |

Total Republican 9 votes

| Total BI | 3 | 7 | 6 | 5 |

Total Bipartisan 21 votes

R or D = Majority of one party voted in support of (against the majority of the other party)
BI = Bipartisan vote (majority of both parties voted "Yea")
).

---

[1] Wilson, 2006.

[2] Mercier, S.S. 2011. "External Factors that will drive the next Farm Bill debate." *Choices.*; Gilbert, J. and Oladi R. 2012. "Net Campaign Contributions, Agricultural Interests, and Votes on Liberalizing Trade with China." *Public Choice* 150:745-769.; Hurwitz, Mark S., Roger J. Moiles and David W. Rohde. 2001. Distributive and Partisan Issues in Agricultural Policy in the 104th House," *American Political Science Review* 95:911-922.; Lee, Frances E. 2008. "Dividers, Not Uniters: Presidential Leadership and Senate Partisanship, 1981-2004." *Journal of Politics* 70:914-928.

[3] Mercier, S.S. 2011. "External Factors that will drive the next Farm Bill debate." *Choices.*

[4] Abler, David. 1989. "Vote Trading on Farm Legislation in the U.S. House." *American Journal of Agricultural Economics.* 71:583-591.; Outlaw, Joe L., James W. Richardson, Steven L. Klose. 2011.

"Farm Bill Stakeholders: Competitors or Collaborators?" Choices 26 (2)
http://www.choicesmagazine.org.
[5] Weingast, Barry. 1979. "A Rational Choice Perspective on Congressional Norms." *American Journal of Political Science* 23:245-262.
[6] Lowi, Theodore J. 1964. "How the farmers get what they want," *Reporter* May 21, 1964 pp. 34-37.
[7] Hurwitz, Mark S., Roger J. Moiles and David W. Rohde. 2001. Distributive and Partisan Issues in Agricultural Policy in the 104th House," *American Political Science Review* 95:911-922.; Lee, Frances E. 2008. "Dividers, Not Uniters: Presidential Leadership and Senate Partisanship, 1981-2004." *Journal of Politics* 70:914-928.; Odum, Lance L. 2012. "Partisan Politics, Agricultural Interests and Effects on State-level Ethanol Subsidies." Open SIUC Research Papers. Paper 324.
http://opensiuc.lib.siu.edu/gs_rp/324
[8] Shiengate, 2001.
[9] Krutz, Glen S. 2005. "Issues and Institutions: 'Winnowing' in the U.S. Congress." *American Journal of Political Science* 49:313-326.
[10] Imhoff, Daniel. 2012. *Food Fight: The Citizen's Guide to the Next Food and Farm Bill* (2nd). Healdsburg, CA: Watershed Media.
[11] Nestle, Marion. 2013. *Food Politics: How the Food Industry Influences Nutrition and Health* (3rd) Berkeley, CA: University of California Press.
[12] Lusk, Jayson. 2013. *The Food Police: A Well-fed Manifesto About the Politics of Your Plate.* New York: Crown Forum.
[13] Bosso, Christopher. 2017. *Framing the Farm Bill: Interests, Ideology and the Agricultural Act of 2014.* University Press of Kansas.
[14] e.g., Shiengate, 2001; Lusk 2013.
[15] Shiengate, 2001.
[16] Hurwitz, Mark S., Roger J. Moiles and David W. Rohde. 2001. Distributive and Partisan Issues in Agricultural Policy in the 104th House," *American Political Science Review* 95:911-922.
[17] Vogel, David. 1989. *Fluctuating Fortunes: The Political Power of Business in America.* New York: Basic Books.
[18] Mercier 2011.
[19] Outlaw et al. 2011.
[20] Gillickson, Gil. 2017. "How Tough Times May Key a Better Farm Bill," Successful Farming Magazine September 2017
[21] E.g., Fiorina, Morris P. 2004. "What ulture Wars?" *Wall Street Journal.* July 14, 2004.; Wilson, James Q. 2006. "How Divided Are We? *Commentary* February 2006.
[22] Seabrook, Andrea. 2010. "CQ: 2009 Was the Most Partisan Year Ever." NPR January 11, 2010. http://www.npr.org
[23] Ball, Molly. 2014. "How Republicans Lost the Farm." *The Atlantic.* January 27, 2014.
[24] Wilde, Parke E. 2014. "After Long Argument, Then Compromise, Congress Agrees on Nutrition Assistance Benefit Cuts in the Agricultural Act of 2014." *Choices* 29(2). http://www.choicesmagazine.org
[25] Outlaw et al. 2011; Mercier 2011
[26] Ball 2014
[27] Hurwitz, Moiles, Rohde 2001; Schlesinger, Joseph A. 1975. "The Primary Goals of Political Parties: A Clarification of Positive Theory." *American Political Science Review* 69: 840-9.
[28] Outlaw et al. 2011
[29] Mooney, Chris Z. 2000. "The Decline of Federalism and the Rise of Morality-Policy Conflict in the United States. *Publius.* 30:171-188.; Meier, Kenneth J. 2001. *The Public Clash of Private Values: The Politics of Morality Policy.* Chatham, NJ: Chatham House.
[30] E.g., Plein, L. Christopher. 1991. "Popularizing Biotechnology: The Influence of Issue Definition." *Science, Technology & Human Values* 16:474-490.; Webber, David J. 1995. "The Emerging Federalism of U.S. Biotechnology Policy." *Politics and the Life Sciences* 14:65-72.; Imhoff 2012;

Hand, Michael S., and Stephen Martinez. 2010. "Just What does Local Mean?" Choices 25 (1) http://www.choicesmagazine.org ; Lusk, 2013. Hopkinson, Jenny. 2014. "Monsanto Confronts Devilish Public Image Problem." *Politico* November 29, 2013 http://dyn.politico.com ; Stephan, Hannes R. 2014. *Cultural Politics and the Transatlantic Divide over GMO's*. New York: Palgrave Macmillan.; Confessore, Nicholas. 2014. "How School Lunch Became the Latest Political Battleground." *The New York Times*. October 7, 2014.; Harris, Rebecca C. 2016. The Political Identity of Food: Partisan Implications of the New Food Politics." Food Studies: An Interdisciplinary Journal 6(4):1-20.

[31] Sheingate 2001, Nestle 2013

[32] Tweeten, Luther. 2003. *Terrorism, Radicalism, and Populism in Agriculture*. Ames, IA: Iowa State Press.

[33] Hurwitz, Moiles, Rohde 2001; Schlesinger 1975

[34] Gonzalez, Sarah. 2012. "Agri-Pulse Poll shows most farmers will vote Romney, blame Democrats on Farm Bill." *Agri-Pulse* 11-5-12.

[35] Schafer, Sam. 2012. "Nearly 200 Farmers share voting intentions." *Farm Journal* 10-18-12.

36 Bump, Philip. 2014. "There really are Two Americas. An Urban one and a Rural one." *The Washington Post* October 21, 2014.

[37] Agri-pulse. Support for Trump Eroding in Farm Country. March 21, 2018. https://www.agri-pulse.com/articles/10743-farmers-and-ranchers-still-like-trump-but-support-eroded

[38] World Public Opinion. 2009. "Americans Oppose Most Farm Subsidies" *World Public Opinion*. April 22, 2009. http://www.worldpublicopinion.org

[39] Gallup. 2011. "Americans Oppose Cuts in Education, Social Security and Defense." Gallup Poll Report January 26, 2011. http://www.gallup.com/poll/145790

[40] Lauinger, John. 2018. "Poll Indicates some support for farm subsidies" Politico 7-30-2018 https://www.politico.com/story/2018/07/30/poll-indicates-some-support-for-farm-subsidies-749870

[41] One method of identifying party differences is to examine "patterns of opposition between the two parties" (Dunlap, Riley E., and Micheal Patrick Allen. 1976. "Partisan Differences on Environmental Issues: A Congressional Roll-Call Analysis." *Western Political Quarterly* 29:384-397.). Defined as party line votes, these are votes where a majority of one party opposes a majority of the other party. "Roll call votes are considered partisan if a majority of Democrats vote against a majority of Republicans." (Souva, Mark, and David Rohde. 2007. "Elite Opinion Differences and Partisanship in Congressional Foreign Policy, 1975-1996," Political Research Quarterly 60:113-123.).

[42] House and Senate versions can be quite partisan in their content. For instance, the 2014 farm bill had provisions to strip $40 billion from SNAP in the House (R-controlled) and only $4 billion in the Senate (D-controlled), and both bills differed on adjusted gross income limits and total subsidy caps for recipients of subsidy programs.

[43] Haskell 2010; Hurwitz et al. 2001.

[44] Scholars attribute this largely to log-rolling and disproportionate minority (farm) interest on agricultural committees (Hurwitz et al. 2001; Gilbert & Oladi 2012; Plumer 2013; Freshwater and Leising 2015). However, many commentators feel this cannot last, and that ideology will eventually split food and agriculture policy along partisan lines (Mercier 2011; Ball 2014). These commentators focus on the partisan rhetoric and partisan chamber votes on partisan issues such as poverty support and fiscal responsibility. Congressional roll-call data seem to support both views.

Chapter 7

Reading the Menu: Party Platforms and Food Politics

We have looked at the players on the field, such as presidents or members of Congress. We have seen them plan their games and we have seen them compete for a spot on the field. We have seen what they do when they are on the field, such as veto farm bills or vote in stronger SNAP and conservation spending. However, is there any way to know what is on the menu before we commit? Can we *see* their food policy goals and ideas *ahead of time?* Luckily we can. We can read their party platform (like a policy menu) to know exactly what they plan or hope to serve up for policy dinner.

Political parties publish extensive policy menus for voters—even if most voters never read them! (Which always surprises me. It is like asking for the Chef's Surprise based on campaign ads and stump speeches alone—Why not read the whole menu?) Furthermore, these menus are collective, meaning the entire party is committed to policy in these directions. It also means there will be pushback from by rogue players or candidates who fail to toe the party line. So voters shouldn't just order "the usual"—they should see what their parties are up to when they vote.

But what if we really look at the politics menu and see what they plan to serve, if elected? Menus do more than list dishes to be served. Like most menus, the party platforms give us a sense of the Chef's philosophy and approach to policy cooking and the actual reasons or values behind that cooking. Party "menus" have different sections for different "courses" and it might be extensive or quite limited in each part—it might even be based on the "daily catch" of crises or issues that election cycle.

When it comes to food policy in contemporary times, Republicans have much more extensive food policy menus than Democrats. Republicans lay out their food policy values, their philosophy, and numerous agenda items and policy goals for consideration. Democrats seem to offer food policy as an afterthought, perhaps assuming voters don't have room for dessert after they work on all the other tasty progressive portions in the platform. Republicans, by contrast, have made food and farming policy part of the main course in their policy agenda, making "Agriculture" a major plank in their 2016 platform. 2016 Democrats offered only a cursory "glance" at farm issues, food policy or rural development—forcing this scholar to "dig" to find out what they had on the menu anyway.

So who is the Farmer's Party? Up until now it would seem as if the Democratic Party is more likely to offer farmers a strong economic safety net and ongoing consumer subsidies for the food industry in the form of SNAP benefits, school lunches and other nutrition programming. Republican presidents and party leadership in Congress have consistently sought to reduce federal farm programs and nutrition funding across the board, making them seem like an unlikely candidate for "Farmer's Party."

However, when we look at the commitments of the political parties to farmers, a very different picture of the realities back at the barn comes into focus. In recent times, that barn has become a political battleground, with government involved in every part of the farm, not just the bank account. The EPA is overseeing site permits and ditch regulations for the barnyard and surrounding fields. The US Forest Service and Bureau of Land Management have expanded protected areas and reduced grazing. Water rights have been curtailed for operations dependent on decades-old agricultural irrigation projects. State laws have overturned centuries of animal husbandry practices. Farm labor has become heavily regulated beyond traditional arrangements. Rural lending agencies have vanished in the wake of burdensome anti-Wall Street bank regulations. Estate Taxes require the next generation of farmers to sell the farm to pay the taxes. Even progressive farmers find themselves hamstrung by food safety laws for produce, inspection laws for butchering, and regulations against raw milk. The list goes on. While farming is a way of life, it is also a business. As a business, the regulatory burdens of the modern regulatory state have become front and center concerns to farmers and their families—and this means Republicans prominently feature it in their menu.

This is not new, but it is different. While freedom to farm loosened the USDA regulation of farm quotas for most commodities in the mid-1990's, government still controls pricing indirectly with continued subsidy structures for minimum prices for many commodities. Furthermore, bureaus and agencies tasked with protecting workers and the environment see farming as the last frontier in industrial regulation, and farmers balk at being regulated like an industrial manufacturer. The majority of American farms (96%) are family farms and most are modest operations, and they may struggle under regulatory burdens designed for corporate structures. In this spirit, the Republican Party, as the party of industry, has appealed to the free enterprise, business-end of farming. It has also appealed to the family-end of farming on cultural and social matters, as many farm families possess traditional orientations to family and work.

Furthermore, if farm policy is no longer "welfare" policy, it may not truly be at home in the party of the New Deal (Democrats). As this chapter will demonstrate, there has been a realignment of farm interests to business interests. Farm policy is no longer a family welfare policy, causing food and farm interests to part ways in the Democratic and Republican parties of today.

Party Platforms and Party Politics

Picture a stadium and the one thing you cannot help but notice are the colors, especially competing colors. Red team fans sport the same red team colors of the players and coaching staff. Blue team fans wear blue team paraphernalia in solidarity with the blue colors of the players and coaches. Even the goals and field markings usually reflect team colors, and that is our focus on in this chapter. We want to understand what the players and coaching staff are really after. Where do their strategies and plays lead us in the food world? What is the goal of the blue team for food and agriculture policy? How is it different from the goal of the red team?

Handily, we can step off the field and head to the meeting rooms of the coaching staff to find out. They do not keep their playbook a secret (at least not officially, though a few skeptics often feel there may be a shadow game played just below the surface), publishing it as the official party platform every four years. The party platform develops and puts forth the positions of party representatives, describing the "issues, principles and goals" of the party.[1]

Leaving conspiracy theories behind, we will take for granted that the platform, the team's playbook or "menu", is a fairly accurate representation of Democratic and Republican policy goals. If we want to know the goals of each team, the party platforms seem like a logical place to start.

Table 8. Major Planks in Party Platforms 2016

Democratic Party Platform 2016
Preamble... "We are Stronger Together"
Raise Incomes and Restore Economic Security for the Middle Class
    Workers, homeownership, social security and retirement
Create Good-paying Jobs
    Infrastructure, clean energy, research/technology, small business,
    young people
Fight for Economic Fairness and Against Equality
    Fix Wall Street, Promote completion, wealthy taxes, fair trade
Bring Americans together and Remove Barriers for Opportunity
    Racism, criminal justice, immigration, civil rights, urban development,
    arts & culture
    Investing in Rural America ***
    Ending poverty and investing in communities left behind ***
Protect Voting Rights, Fix our Campaign Finance System and Restore our
Democracy
Combat Climate Change, Build a Clean Energy Economy, Secure Environmental
Justice
    Protect our public lands
Provide Quality and Affordable Education
    Free college, student debt relief, predatory for-profit colleges,
    universal pre-school
Ensure the Health and Safety of All Americans
    Universal health care, drug costs, addiction, mental health, Autism,
    long-term care, guns
Principled Leadership
Support our Troops and Keep Faith with our Veterans
Confront Global Threats
Protect our Values
A leader in the World

Republican Party Platform 2016
Preamble "We believe in American Exceptionalism"
Restoring the American Dream
> *Taxes, trade policy, financial markets, homeownership, transportation,*
> *technology, electric grid*
> *Workplace freedom, reducing federal debt*

Rebirth of Constitutional Government
> *We the people rule, judiciary, administrative law, marriage, first*
> *amendment, guns, privacy, life,*
> *Private property, intellectual property rights, federalism, elections*

America's Natural Resources: Agriculture, Energy and the Environment
> *Abundant harvests and farm policy, Energy policy, Environmental*
> *Progress* ***

Government Reform
> *Balanced Budget, preserving Medicare & Medicaid, social security,*
> *internet freedom,*
> *Immigration, treaties, IRS, Pentagon, federal workforce, term limits,*
> *corporate welfare*

Great American Families, Education, Healthcare, Criminal Justice
America Resurgent

To get a sense of the Playbook, just look at the Table of Contents from each team's platform (See Table 8.) Republicans did not publish a new platform in 2020, so 2016 is the best year for comparison. The Table lists the Major and minor 2016 "planks" in each platform, and it is easy to get a sense of priorities from just the order of the playbook. Think of a *plank* as the key piece used to build a *platform* to stand on. That is the idea behind *planks* and *platforms*. So what are the Democrats standing on? Democrats lead with incomes, economic security, jobs, economic fairness and civil rights—moving on to voting rights, climate change, education, health, military, global threats and American foreign policy. Buried in the civil rights section called "Barriers to Opportunity" is a section called Investing in Rural America. This is the part of the Democratic playbook most focused on food and farming. It is also telling that food policy becomes an investment in a community and couched in the language of opportunity, notably next to the section on poverty and communities left behind. Democrats still see rural policy, food policy and farm policy as part of welfare policy.

By contrast, Republicans stand on Agriculture as a major plank in their platform. Republicans see Agriculture as a family-oriented business extracting necessities from the earth. After discussing taxes, trade, debt, Republicans focus on constitutional rights of religious freedom, speech, bearing arms, privacy, property, and other conservative values. After that, the party turns to "Americas

Natural Resources" to discuss agriculture, energy and the environment. The discussion of agriculture praises farmers and ranchers for their Abundant Harvests, and then focuses on technical business issues: trade, diary supports, livestock marketing, food and menu labels, EPA farm regulation and water rights, risk management and farm data. A separate plank in the platform calls for separating farm policy from welfare policy with an explicit call to "separate the administration of SNAP" from the USDA. Clearly, Republicans are concerned with the regulation of agriculture *as a business*, a far different approach than Democrats.

So where did this platform come from and who wrote it? Party platforms are written every four years and they are adopted at each party's national convention, often literally held in a sports stadium. Delegates from each state attend meetings earlier in the year to represent and hammer out the playbook and get together at the end of the summer choose the first-string players for the team. The Party Convention itself is literally a summer meeting of "the coaching staff" deciding who to "start" in the presidential election game and to approve the team's playbook. The meeting isn't really a pre-season meeting because the presidential election game has been underway for months, as players visit fans in the various states hoping for the nomination nod when those fans vote in the primary elections. In the election of 2016, the blue team had a long pre-season fight between former Secretary of State Hillary Clinton and Sen. Bernie Sanders. The Red team, even more spectacularly, had an upstart outsider player, Donald Trump, run away with the fans, leaving the veteran players and early favorites on the bench.

While recent conventions may not seem to have much to do with food politics, one of the key lessons of farm politics and party food has been the *centrality* of farm concerns to party concerns in American history. Today's media may make food and farming seem like a fringe issue in government, but earlier Americans would have understood it to be a much more mainstream affair. In fact, some of the more colorful lore of party conventions directly relates to farm policy. This chapter will compare party platforms, but first some context.

Stadium Stories: Seating Delegates and Designing Platforms

Before we even look at the playbook itself, let's consider who is on staff and how they got there. *Who* is the political party, at its heart? Political scientists do not give much credence to the fans in the stands. Political parties are not groups of citizens, at least not in any official sense. Rather, political scientists consider the American political party to be, at its core, the players and the coaching staff. And, in reality, they consider the heart to be the players and those in the coaching staff *who want to be players*. According to political scientist, John Aldrich, "Who then are these critical actors [at convention]? It is political leaders—those who seek or hold political office—who are the central actors in the party."[2]

Thus our work so far has been looking in right places for partisan activity and food policy. We correctly examined the players on the field, Congressmen and presidents. However, unlike sports, where most coaches are *former* players, in political parties many party activists (our "coaching staff") *aspire to be* players. This could be anyone from the senior party official hoping for a nod in a big office (e.g., Terry McAuliffe, Democratic Party Chair and Clinton friend who obtained a nomination and subsequent election to the governorship of Virginia) to the lowly college student campaign volunteer, hoping to network for a congressional staff position.

As one might expect, farmers and food activists are not the primary players at these conventions. Today, very few farmers and even fewer foodies seek personal political office or influence, but they do exist. Historically, farmers played a much bigger role in American politics, with prominent founding fathers such as George Washington, Thomas Jefferson, John Adams, James Madison and many others having significant agricultural enterprises and seeking to demonstrate farm business leadership to the nation with experiments on their farms.

Getting a Seat at the Table

As we know, the convention is there to nominate a candidate for the presidency. For our purposes, we will dig deeper into what *else* happens at convention. Two other steps are fascinating to consider in light of food policy history. First, there is the incredibly controversial decision to decide who can be "seated" and given official credentials to be part of the party convention. Occasionally states have sent conflicting delegations, both vying to be recognized as the official partisan delegation from a given state, and some of these credentialing fights have been related to farm policy. In a famous fight in the election of 1848, the Democratic Party had to decide which New York delegation to seat, the Barnburners (progressive, anti-slavery wing) or the Hunkers (the conservative New York democrats). The compromise was to seat half-and-half, but the Barnburners walked out, and the Hunkers refused to participate. In response, the Barnburners went on to form their own team, the Free-Soil Party, to compete for Democratic votes in the general election. The 1852 platform of the Free-Soil party called for the U.S. to hold its public lands in trust, granting portions only to "landless settlers" (even immigrants) for *free*, rather than selling land to corporations, especially railroads. They also called for "river and harbor improvements" to facilitate commerce and trade, especially for agricultural products in the new frontier. Free Soil was also an abolitionist party with many members joining the Republicans after the 1952 election.

Players Writing Playbooks

The second part of the convention, even more important to us, is the development of the official party platform—the document which acts as a sort of playbook for the players and the coaches. Again, in contrast to sports, political players get to write their own plays. A select committee from among the delegates drafts the playbook at special meetings over the course of the year, presenting the finished document to the convention for a vote. In the 2016 election, these committees were almost exclusively officeholders—Senators, Representatives, and Governors—and aspiring players, such as Ms. Kelly Armstrong, who co-wrote the Republican Party Agriculture section. Armstrong went on to win the GOP House Primary seat for North Dakota in 2018, unseating the incumbent and winning the seat in a state where farming interests still occupy much of the time and energy of its members in Congress. On the Democratic side, co-chairs of the committee were pushed aside so that candidates Hillary Clinton and Bernie Sanders could choose who sat on the committee, and the official document does not tell us who wrote the Rural Life section.

Sometimes, the players on the field really write the platform. When the incumbent president is seeking reelection, It is common for the White House to submit a draft platform to the committee as a starting point. The idea is that the team should continue to move the ball according to the direction indicated by the current prominent player, the president and the Administration once they are on the field. But this does not always happen. However, yet again, another fascinating story from farmland turns this convention (no pun intended) on its head.

You may remember that 1896 was the year of the Cinderella team, the Populist Party, stealing victories in state races. One of their issues was the gold standard of the Democratic Incumbent Grover Cleveland and a demand for free silver. The Democratic convention and platform tried to reach out to populist demands, so populists would vote for Democrats. True to form, the convention met in the Chicago Coliseum. William Jennings Bryan was a Democrat and a Nebraska Populist supporter. While his delegation was not seated at the convention (in one of those seating fights so common in conventions), in favor of the Nebraska Gold Standard supporters, Bryan was invited to give a speech in support of free silver for the debate on the monetary platform of the Democratic Party. His speech chastised Cleveland by claiming "we should not crucify mankind on a cross of gold." While he had worked for months behind the scenes for the nomination, the speech galvanized the convention and propelled him to the nomination for president via a vote on the floor. As a Congressman from Nebraska, he understood the monetary issue as a farm economy issue. The gold standard kept money in tight supply, making it hard to pay back debts. The entire nation had been a severe depression 1893-1896, with farmers losing their land when they could not pay back their debts. In an amazing sweep, William Jennings

Bryan emerged as the Democratic nominee, stealing the nomination from the incumbent president! (Jennings had worked behind the scenes to curry favor with insiders for months, and his victory over Cleveland at the convention is one of the major political party stories in American History.)

Another good story about rogue players centers squarely on farm politics. Republican President Donald Trump famously ran the ball the other way on free trade when he took office, refusing to move forward with the TPP negotiated by Obama and starting a tariff war with our major trading partners. Both actions directly impacted farm prospects by limiting opportunities to sell and grow new markets abroad for American commodities. Since free trade is a plank in the Republican Party Platform, one might have expected the other red players on the field to stick with the game plan and block his plays literally with an Act of Congress, but the Republicans seemed to fear the fans in the stands demanding that the party "Make America Great Again."

In response to the trade war's farm casualties, the Republican Congress actually supported President Trump's $12 billion bailout for farmers in the summer of 2018! Incredibly Trump's USDA was able to put out a press release of prominent Republicans, such as the House Agriculture Committee Chair, supporting the bailout![3] (An op-ed from the American Farm Bureau supported the bailout too, but noted farmers "prefer trade to aid".[4]) A savvy reader should already see through this as an expert. "Yes, Professor Harris, but that was the Farm Bloc supporting the bailout, not the mainstream Republican Party in Congress. What did Republican Speaker Ryan say?" The savvy reader would be correct that Speaker Ryan tried to limit the damage to mainstream party goals by calling it a "short term" fix and calling for an end to the Trump tariff war.[5]

Making a Team Playbook and a Winning Platform

Whether the committee or the White House take the lead to write the platform, the challenge has been to create a document the entire party can get behind, especially one that will serve the needs of all teammates (party candidates) seeking office. For this reason, party platforms have been understood to be quite watered down affairs, with little hard facts and policies. That said, political scientists tend to examine party platforms in a manner which sorts "symbolic" statements from "substantive" statements, finding most platforms to be a fairly even mix.[6]

For our purposes, we are interested in both food and farm ideas and particular food and farm policies that motivate contemporary Democrats and Republicans. Again, since this isn't a novel, I will tell you the outcome up front. Political scientists generally expect party platforms to move towards each other, rather than away from each other.[7] In other words, they often "converge" and land at the same place on many issues. It may seem as if we can picture the field in reverse, with the red and blue painted goals in the center and the teams moving from fringe to center, their goals right next to each other! This is because the fans in the stands tend to also be "in the center" on most things, so parties will move to "capture" the center or "median" voter. Sure a few fans may prefer radical red or blue policy (out in right or left field!), but most Americans prefer more centrist approaches to most problems. This is part of the story in farm and food policy. Several areas converge, at least in theory. For instance, in the early 1990's environmental and conservation policy was a mainstream concern of most Americans. In that spirit, *both* parties will call for environmental protection and conservation in farm policy and natural resources. The 1996 Republican Freedom to farm bill included the first Conservation Title in an American farm bill precisely due to these nation-wide sentiments. Of course, political scientists also recognize that parties often differ on the specifics, and "diverge" on the appropriate policy response.

Symbolism and Substance

In this spirit, political parties will use *symbolic* and *substantive* gestures in their platforms. The symbolic gestures may converge while the substantive prescriptions diverge. For this reason, we will look at symbolic and substantive partisan statements on food policy. Symbols are powerful because people value them. They also convey a lot of meaning.[8] The key difference between the two is that substantive policy statements actually lay out the exact government response to an issue. On the other hand, symbolic statements reassure the public of the sympathy and values the party to a particular concern or belief.

Sponsors Spoiling the Fun

Another twist in the story is that political scientists generally expect the party to be quite out of touch with this center due to the sponsors, the organized interests behind each party. These sponsors typically control the players, which means they control the convention and "will strive to recruit and elect candidates sympathetic to their goals, goals typically not shared by most ordinary voters."[9] Because of this, it is quite possible to see very divergent and even outlier positions emerge in party platforms, such as a provision on food labels or a call to reduce livestock.

The 2016 Playbook

As the political parties took their positions on the field in 2016, they had very different plays in mind for food and agriculture policy in the U.S. They also emphasized different symbolic values to appeal to their fans. The Democratic Platform devoted much less space, 90% less space, than the Republicans to food and agriculture discussions, perhaps already hinting that food and agriculture policy is much more of a priority to Republicans than to Democrats. Furthermore, the Democratic platform provided only symbolic lip-service promises to traditional farm and food concerns whereas the Republican platform was much more substantive and detailed in nature. Indeed, the entire 2016 Republican Platform reads like a fortune teller's view of 2017, 2018 and beyond. The Republican team read the playbook and made each play in lockstep with their platform, and the food policy (and other policy) served up was the exact same food on the menu!

Democratic Food Values

The 2016 Democratic Platform tackled most of its farm plays in a section called "Investing in Rural America" –a two paragraph miniscule subsection of a behemoth promise to address the civil rights and opportunities concerns of sixteen separate groups. The word *farmers* occurs only twice in the entire document, and the word *farm* only once. Even the *rural* was referenced only once outside of this section, in the context of small business opportunities. Of all the platforms examined for this project, this particular platform was noteworthy for its clear marginalization of farmers and farm interests. Even "food" took a back seat mentioned only four times, twice in the context of local food, once in a SNAP section discussing the need to help "struggling" families "put food on the table", and once in the context of food safety and international trade agreements. The only other noteworthy piece for farm interests was a section on "Reining in Wall Street" and a promise to give the "Commodity Futures Commission" more enforcement resources.

In their playbook, the Democrats begin their call for a "stronger rural and agricultural economy" by focusing on more funding for sustainable farming and more protection for "family farms". They also project to grow the rural economy through "local food markets" and "regional food systems" and "clean energy leadership" as well as "water, sewer and broadband infrastructure." In a nod to more traditional farm programs they promise to "provide a focused safety net to assist family operations that need support during challenging times." That is all. No details of any kind for any of these largely symbolic statements. By contrast, the DNC platform of 2000 provided a laundry list of farm policy goals, infrastructure promises, including internet, and a promise to undo the "misguided" Republican "Freedom to Farm" policy. Gone are the days when parity payments and technical, substantive food policy plays could be found in Democratic platforms. The only policy promise approaching substantive support was a promise to "double loan guarantees" (double the price) for government subsidized biomass products. Even the section on the Supplemental Nutrition Assistance Program (food stamps) promised only to "protect" the policy as "our nation's most important anti-hunger program." There were no details on what that might mean for the average beneficiary.

Further concerns raised in the DNC platform follow the civil rights and opportunity theme of the playbook, and are notably more detailed. They note the need to protect "farmworkers" and tout the EPA's Agricultural Worker Protection Standard as a safety achievement. They also call for stronger protections of farm labor: "regulation of work hours, elimination of child labor, ensuring adequate housing for migrant workers and sanitary facilities in the fields"—all echoing traditional labor concerns. They note the need to support "young farmers and ranchers" –a group currently supported under USDA programs for farm opportunity. They note their support for the "marijuana industry" including, presumably, the growing of marijuana and for the "clean fuels" and biomass products. They also single out "agricultural lands" for their environmental impact claiming "we must enlist farmers as partners in promoting conservation and change."

Republicans, the Farmer's Party

Republicans, by comparison, prominently feature agriculture in their menu. "We are the party of America's growers, producers, farmers, ranchers foresters, miners, commercial fishermen, and all those who bring from the earth the crops, minerals, energy, and the bounties of our seas that are the lifeblood of our economy." In stark contrast the lack of emphasis on farm policy in the Democratic platform, the Republicans spelled out a myriad of substantive policy goals in 16 dense, lengthy paragraphs. The Republicans gave Agriculture top billing in the third major plank of the party's playbook. This section has its own mini-preamble, praising farmers for their "labor and ingenuity and love of the land [which] feeds billions of people around the world." Aptly praising the "abundant harvests" of American agriculture, the Republicans note that we feed ourselves more cheaply than anywhere in the world, that we give more food aid than any other nation on earth as the "largest agricultural exporter in the world." From this vantage point, the Republicans launch into a list of detailed policy planks:

- Expanding trade and new markets
- Opposition to "Depression" era federal dairy policies
- Opposition to "draconian rules" for livestock and poultry marketing
- Opposition to "intrusive and expensive federal mandates on food options and menu labeling" opposition to mandatory labeling of GMO food "proven safe and healthy"
- Opposition to additional regulation of agriculture "particularly from the EPA" and the "travesty" of the "Waters of the U.S. Rule" and a call to devolve environmental protection to the states, making the EPA a federal bureau
- A call for "conservation policies based on the preservation of working land" especially public grazing lands
- Abundant water supply for farmers
- Cost-effective risk management
- A timely farm bill
- Work requirements for able-bodied SNAP recipients
- A call to separate the administration of SNAP from the Department of Agriculture
- Data protection and private ownership for farm data on commercial software
- Properly managed timber to control fires and pests
- Limiting Endangered Species listings that "threaten to devastate farmers and ranchers"

The Republican platform also had symbolic nods to hard work, private property, farm families and even detailed their commitment to these interests. Republicans come across in this section of the document as pro-farm, pro-business, pro-forest, pro-meat, pro-GMO, and pro free-market food.

However, we might should not jump to hasty conclusions. Buried elsewhere in the platform are references to older debates. Of note is the old farm problem of the gold standard and currency, something farmers as debtors and the Republican Party have historically differed on. The 2016 platform calls for "sound money rather than political pressure for easy money and loose credit" and a consideration of the "plausibility of a metallic basis for U.S. currency." This plank harkens back to the old days of the call for a gold standard loathed by many debtor-farmer interests. Also, there is also no mention of support for a farm safety net or farm subsidies, a traditional bone-of-contention for free-market conservatives, and there is a veiled reference to "federal dairy policies, crafted during the Great Depression", as an "impediment" to growth, a likely criticism of the federal milk price supports. Furthermore, the support for "risk management and insurance" cautiously notes, "it should be effective." Republicans still do not want to spend "easy" money to keep farmers afloat.

Republicans also noted agriculture in other sections of their platform. One area of concern was access to credit and technology. In a section on "Freeing Financial Markets" Republicans noted the toll of "heavy federal regulation" on community banks, banks responsible for the "majority of agricultural loans and small business loans." In a later section on Small Business and Entrepreneurship, they also noted these banks provide "three quarters of all agricultural loans." In a section on technology, Republicans noted how the lack of "universal broadband coverage...hurts rural America, where farmers, ranchers and small business people need connectivity."

Another concern was balancing conservation, environmental protection, and property rights. In a section on The Fifth Amendment: Protecting Private Property, Republicans spoke of government takings including "the taking of water rights" and the taking of property by environmental regulations that destroy or diminish the property's value. By the time Republicans get to their Agriculture platform, they are decrying the "regulatory juggernaut, particularly from the EPA" and the EPA's Waters of the US (WOTUS) rule. "We must never allow federal agencies to seize control of state waters, watersheds, or groundwater the control of sovereign states." In the very next breath, Republicans state "Farmers and ranchers are among this country's leading conservationists" who "reduce erosion, improve water and air quality, and increase wildlife habitat" through USDA conservation policies (These programs require farmers receiving any USDA benefits to file an NRC-approved conservation plan and comply with that plan. The programs also subsidize environmental and wildlife set-asides, land that is not farmed in order to provide environmental benefits.) In terms of public lands, Republicans pledge to protect "working lands" stating "ranching on public lands must be fostered, developed and encouraged." In this spirit, they also support "an abundant water supply for America's farmers, ranchers and their communities."

In stark contrast to Democrats, the Republican platform takes them personally to task for their SNAP endeavors:

> The Democrats play politics with farm security [by delaying the 2014 farm bill]. Much of the delay had nothing to do with the vital role of American agriculture. It concerned their efforts to expand welfare through SNAP, which now comprises more than 70 percent of all farm bill spending. During the last eight years of a Democratic Administration, nearly all of the work requirements for able-bodied adults...have been removed. We will restore those provisions and, to correct a mistake when the food stamp program was first created in 1964, separate the administration of SNAP from the Department of Agriculture.

Anything New on the Menu?

Issues mentioned only in 2016 by either party also demonstrate new frontiers in food policy: Young Farmers and Ranchers was a program developed in the 2014 farm bill as a response to the aging farm population (average age of a farmer 55 down from 65). The program, specifically mentioned in the Democratic platform, subsidizes loans and provides support programs for farmers under 40 who have farmed less than ten years. Commodity futures regulation, another new addition to the Democratic platform, a by-product of Wall Street reform since the Great Recession. By contrast, Republicans listed a host of statements against proposals and programs pursued by the previous (Democratic) administration to further regulate the "business" of farming: Menu labeling, Livestock and Poultry Marketing regulations, GMO labels, and the WOTUS EPA rule. Republicans also stated their support for the private ownership of farm data, to answer a concern of farmers using GPS in new equipment and who owns the farm data generated by that equipment. While some of these issues have roots in the New Deal divide over proper government reach into the farm economy, some represent issues arising from demographic, technology and financial instrument/corporate trends.

Taking a look at the 2016 Democratic and Republican Discussions of farming and food, it is not too hard to see which party is more the farmer's party. But has this always been the case? And what about "Foodies"—where are their interests? Neither party seems to have much to say in 2016 about food consumer interests, though the Democratic Party seemed to have more to say, at least symbolically. The support for local food and regional food, as well as a commitment to "food safety" in trade, provide at least some lip-service to potential foodie issues. No details for any of these ideas are presented. For their part, Republicans focus on the consumer noting that "Americans spend a smaller percentage of their income on food than any other nation" as part of their "Abundant Harvests" message.

Red Food, Blue Food: Party Platforms and Food and Agricultural Policy

Food and Agriculture policy encompasses a broad range of policies and concerns for party platforms. While party platforms have been viewed with skepticism by scholars,[10] they still represent a somewhat reliable sense of the party's thinking on issues [11] and reputational and agenda-setting goals—those symbolic and substantive statements we saw in 2016. For the reader interested in a more complete technical analysis, this section presents a side-by-side comparison of food policy and party platforms since 1992 provides a more comprehensive view of Democrats, Republicans, Food and Farming in recent times.

Party platforms from 1992-2016 can be analyzed and compared for a comprehensive picture of Red and Blue approaches to farm policy. Starting in 1992, parties moved into significantly different ideological camps, nicely sorting into liberal (Democratic) and conservative (Republican) approaches to many policy areas. This cut-point is where the parties significantly diverged and coalesced around separate ideological agendas for the future of the nation. Gone are the days when one could not tell a difference between "Tweedle Dee and Tweedle Dum." However, since food policy has traditionally been more bipartisan, we may expect less difference than in other areas. Yet, if we were going to find difference in contemporary policy, this would be the place and time it would emerge.

For that reason, this analysis examined party platforms from 1992-2016 to capture contemporary farm politics, noting each place the party referred to "food, nutrition, farms/farmers/ranchers, rural, and agriculture" and coding the sentence for policy/issue/value and support/non-support. Most food and agricultural policy is contained in a separate sub-section dedicated to agriculture or rural issues, but not always. References to food and agriculture were also found in colorful platform introductions and in sections on poverty, trade, and natural resources. The policies, issues and values coded for approximate many farm bill provisions, but also go beyond the farm bill "fold" to additional concerns (such as estate taxes and private property). Also of note is that, similar to 2016, the Republican Party platforms had at least twice as much text devoted to food and farming.

Table 9 presents a side-by-side comparison of policy/issue/value support in Democratic and Republican platforms. Programs are broken down into major policies for comparison across the years. The chart lists each year and a check-mark for agreement or an X for disagreement. Each policy section is discussed below:

Table 9: Food and Agriculture Policy Support in U.S. Political Party Platforms

POLICY	DEMOCRATIC PLATFORM							REPUBLICAN PLATFORM						
	20 16	20 12	20 08	20 04	20 00	19 96	19 92	20 16	20 12	20 08	20 04	20 00	19 96	19 92
Farm Safety Net	√	√	√	√		√	√		X	X	√	√		X
Freedom to Farm								(√)			√	√	√	
Risk Mgmt/ Insurance		√						√	√	√		√		
Farm Credit/Loans	√							√						√
Free Trade		√	√	√	(√)	√	√		√	√	√	√	√	√
Int'l Food Aid	√	√							√	√				
Infrastructure	√	√					√		√	√	√	√		√
Research & Dev.		√					√			√	√	√		
Science/ Technology			√						√	√		√	√	√
Bio/ Technology				√					√			√	√	√
Energy/ Ethanol	√			√						√	√	√	√	√
Federal/EPA	√	√		√				X	X	X	X	X	X	X
Conservation	√	√		√		√			√	√	√	√	√	√
Natural Resource Dev					X				√			√	√	
Rangelands/ Forest									√			√	√	
Water Rights								√	√			√	√	
Consumer labeling					√									
Food Safety	√					√	√						√	
Food Stamps/SNAP	√	√				√			X			X		
Nutrition// Obes		√	√				√			√				
Farm Taxation								√	√	√		√		√
Corporate farms				X										
Family	√		√								√	√		√

POLICY	DEMOCRATIC PLATFORM							REPUBLICAN PLATFORM						
farms														
Animal Rights														X
Climate Change	√		√		(√)										
Local Food	√		√												
American Dream			√		√										
Hard Work		√			√				√		√	√		√	
Liberty									√						
Private Property									√		√	√	√	√	

NEW IN 2016	DEMOCRATS	NEW IN 2016	REPUBLICANS
Young Farmers	√	Menu Labels	X
Farm workers	√	Livestock Market Reg.	X
"Way of life"	√	GMO Labels	X
Comm. Futures Reg.	√	Pvt. Ownership of farm data	√
		WOTUS	X

Policies were only recorded if specifically mentioned in the context of food, agriculture, or farm policy

√ = Mentioned Favorably / Support for this policy (√) Mentioned in general, implied support for agriculture context

X = Mentioned Unfavorably / Against this policy

If Blank, this issue was not mentioned in this party platform with regard to food or agriculture.

Farm Support and Traditional Commodity Programs

Traditional commodity programs and farm support are labeled under *Farm Safety Net* (direct payments), *Freedom to Farm* (decoupled direct payments), *Risk Management and Crop Insurance*, and *Farm Credit*. As the chart illustrates, there is some conflict in the party platforms over farm safety-net approaches and the more free-market approach of freedom to farm. Democrats have been very consistent in stating their emphatic support for "A strong farm safety net" in boiler plate language in every platform 1992-2016. By contrast, Republicans in 2008 and 2012 called for "an end to direct payments", and they indeed pursued significant farm subsidy reform and cuts in the 2014 and in 2018 farm bill work. Thus, this seems to be one area the party organizations are parting ways.

The other item of note is that Republicans are much more likely to state their support for other farm support programs, such as risk management, subsidized crop insurance and access to credit, though with the recent caveat that "Federal programs to assist farmers managing risk must be as cost-effective as they are functional" (2016). It is possible to read this as keeping farmers in the fold with new instrumentality, more in line with capitalist, free-market, and fiscally responsible mechanisms. By contrast, the Democratic support of a farm safety net is strongly reminiscent of poverty safety-net characterizations, suggesting Democrats still see a role for government in protecting farmers from raw market forces. In an echo of age-old farm needs, both parties consistently support Free Trade and the expansion of Agricultural export markets in every platform.

Environmental Policy, Water and Public Lands

Democrats and Republicans supported vastly different approaches to agriculture policy. This was in the areas of environmental regulation of agriculture, public land use (Natural Resource Development). Democrats stated strong support for federal environmental regulation (air and water pollution) and EPA enforcement. By contrast, Republicans denounced the EPA and federal efforts to control agriculture in every party platform since 1992. This was especially true in 2016 after the EPA in the Obama Administration interpreted the Clean Water Act to allow significant new regulation of waterways, ponds and ditches on the farm under the Waters of the US (WOTUS) rule with Republicans stating: "Unelected Bureaucrats must be stopped… we must never allow federal agencies to seize control of state waters, watersheds or ground water. [These] must remain the purview of the states."

Natural resource development and use on public lands (especially livestock and forestry) represent another fault-line in party platforms. Democratic platforms spoke out against development of public lands, while Republicans vowed to fight for "multiple use" it in 2000 and 1996. Republicans also made a note of their support for rangelands, forest, and agricultural water rights in "Western lands." Instream flow and irrigation uses also take on a partisan flavor, with Republicans staunchly supporting "water rights" in several platforms. In 2016, the Republican platform combined these concerns stating "ranching on public lands must be fostered, developed, and encouraged. This includes providing for an abundant water supply for America's farmers, ranchers and their communities." Some of this was a reaction to the "Sage Brush Rebellion" against earlier Department of Interior and Bureau of Land Management restrictions in the 1980's, a concern that resurfaced under the Obama Administration's expansion of wilderness lands and wildlife refuges with a ranch family protest and standoff at a remote refuge in Eastern Oregon in 2017. Some of it was also a reaction to a series of Western conflicts with environmental and recreational groups over instream flow from water reservoirs originally built for agricultural irrigation. Farmers wanted to ration the water for agricultural use while environmental groups, fishermen, and whitewater rafters wanted more water flowing for wildlife and tourism.

Farm Conservation Programs

In contrast to environmental regulation, land and water use, Republicans stated strong support for "voluntary" farm conservation programs (soil and water), state environmental regulation and the overall value of "stewardship." In 2016, Republicans stated:

> Farmers and ranchers are among this country's leading conservationists. Modern farm practices and technologies, supported by programs from the Department of Agriculture, have led to reduced erosion, improved water and air quality, increased wildlife habitat. The stewardship of the land benefits everyone, and we remain committed to conservation policies based on the preservation, not restriction, of working lands.

Conservation programs administered by the USDA represent voluntary and reimbursed commitments of private land to meet conservation goals to stop erosion, clean water and maintain habitat. In 2014, the bipartisan farm bill also required all farms participating in USDA subsidy, risk management or loan programs to file enforceable farm-level conservation plans supervised by the NRC at the local USDA office. These programs are considered voluntary, cooperative, and compensatory for farm families, making them more palatable from a farm business perspective. Democrats likewise support USDA conservation programs, calling them "sustainable farming programs" in 2008, and these programs represent a place where Democrats and Republicans *both* endorse environmental regulation of farming.

Nutrition, Health and Obesity

Early in the 2000's, both parties were concerned about the health costs of obesity and the benefits of better nutrition. However, after the Obama Administration sought to change the food pyramid to My Plate, reform school lunch via the Healthy Hunger-Free Kids Act of 2010 and pursue caloric menu labeling for restaurants as part of the Affordable Care Act, the parties went their separate ways on this issue. In 2008, the Democratic platform had pledged to pursue "healthy food environments" in schools to reduce childhood obesity. In 2004, the Republican platform dedicated several paragraphs to Children's health, supporting programs in schools focused on physical activity and "nutritious diet" to combat obesity and heart disease.

Of course, poverty programs and food stamps (SNAP) funding is the other place the parties "part" ways. Republicans have consistently sought to reduce SNAP benefits and restrict eligibility. Under the Trump administration, the USDA even proposed outlandish ideas, such as replacing SNAP with "food boxes." The 2018 farm bill negotiations particularly highlighted a Republican desire for stricter work requirements for SNAP beneficiaries who were not elderly or disabled or had small children at home. Every Republican platform since 1992 had promised to seek to reduce SNAP benefits, and the 2016 Farm Bill called for shifting the SNAP program from the USDA to the Department of Health and Human Services. For their part, Democrats promised to "protect proven programs like SNAP--our nation's most important anti-hunger program" in the part of their 2016 platform dedicated to *Ending Poverty*. However, Democrats did not overemphasize support for SNAP in previous platforms, notably missing in a few years, and in 1996 the DNC even supported reducing food stamp fraud and supporting state experiments with food stamp benefits, likely undertaken to reduce criticism as a response to the combative politics of welfare reform pursued in the Clinton years.

Other Issues

In terms of American values in food and agriculture policy, there is evidence of ideological differences. While Democrats focus on the American Dream, Republicans mentioned private property rights and "liberty". Both parties supported the notion of "hard work" in their platforms. The parties separately pursued support for other issues related to food and agriculture. Republicans were notable in their protection of "private property" and their praise of "hard work" in farming contexts. Republicans were consistent in their pursuit of a reduction in estate taxes "so families can keep the family farm." Republicans were also much more likely to state their support for agricultural/ rural infrastructure, research, science and biotechnology, as well as energy and ethanol. For Democrats, local food, family farms, repeated references to the American Dream and protections for farm workers set them apart, as well as warnings about climate change and corporate farms.

Do We Get What We Order?

Considering the 2016 Party Platforms and looking at a larger comparison for the past 30 years is quite telling. When a party is in power, it *does* seek to serve what is on the menu given the approaches of the Clinton, Bush, Obama and Trump administrations and Congresses, some of which was already detailed in the previous chapters. In recent times, we need only to look at the way Trump pursued WOTUS rollback, SNAP work requirements, and reducing the reach of the estate tax to see examples of lock-step service to the playbook. This tells us that political parties matter and that their platforms are a decent guide to the game.

It also tell us that parties are different. While there is evidence of movement to the middle on many issues such as trade or young farmers or USDA risk management programs, the menus really do offer a taste of something different. Most notably this is in terms of environmental policy and nutrition policy—places where the platforms part ways in stark contrast over public land use, water rights, SNAP, school lunch and retail menu labeling. It is also possible to read between the lines on subsidies and farm safety nets to see that Democrats are more supportive than Republicans of direct payments to farmers. These platforms suggest citizens can easily vote their food values if they know where to look and what to look for.

Overall, in term of the political science debate, it appears there is evidence of partisanship and bipartisanship. The partisanship is along the usual lines known of party coalitions (environment, budget/social spending, and natural resource development). The bipartisan support exhibited some interesting lines of agreement or past agreement (free-trade, health/obesity, and farm conservation programs). This analysis supports the notion that where food and agriculture policy intersects with the usual party coalitions lined up on opposing sides (such as becoming an environmental issue or a regulatory issue), it becomes a place where parties "part" ways. Stepping back, it a can also be said that the Republican party is looking out for the interests of the "business" side of food and agriculture policy (access to capital, resources, R&D, property and taxation), while the Democratic party is looking out for the social and environmental side (Farm safety net, Food stamps, EPA regulation of air, water, climate).

---

[1] Oliver and Marion, p. 398.
[2] John H. Aldrich, *Why parties? A Second Look*, U of Chicago Press, 2011, p. 17
[3] USDA Press Release July 24, 2018. "What they are Saying: Support for President Donald J. Trump's Plan to Protect American Farmers from Unjustified Trade Retaliation."
[4] Zippy Duvall, President of the American Farm Bureau Federation. Opposing View Op-Ed: Farmers need USDA Help, USA today, July 25, 2018.
[5] "Ag Department to Send $12 Billion to Farmers hurt by Tariffs." Washington Post. July 24, 2018.
[6] e.g., Willard M. Oliver and Nancy E. Marion. 2008. "Political Party Platforms: Symbolic Politics and Criminal Justice Policy," Criminal Justice Policy Review 19(4):397-413.
[7] Anthony Downs. 1957. *An Economic Theory of Democracy*. New York: Harper and Row.
[8] Definition of symbols: "the communications by political actors to others for a purpose, in which the specific object referred to conveys a larger meaning, typically with emotional, moral or psychological impact [For which] this larger meaning need not be independently or factually true, but will tap into what people want to believe in as true." Edleman 1988 quoted in Oliver and Marion, p. 400.
[9] Bawn, Kathleen et al. 2012. "A Theory of Political Parties: Groups, Policy Demands and Nominations in American Politics," Perspectives on Politics, 10(3):571-597 at 575.
[10] Hershey and Beck, 2004
[11] Cox and McCubbins 1993, 2005

Chapter 8

Voting with your Fork?

I promised to show foodies and farmers where things stand, so this concluding chapter offers a re-cap of key general points and some tips for voting with your fork. It also offers some thoughts for candidates and government officials and an addendum for my social science friends. We opened our discussion with the idea that voting involves participating in elections and choosing among usually partisan candidates. So what do we know *now*?

At the beginning of this book I provided you with *Some Thoughts on Preparing to Read this Book*, and I asked you to consider four realities. First, I asked you to think about what a history of food policy really means, and you learned very quickly that it meant surprisingly *technical* stuff. Second, I told you why political parties matter—they matter because politics happens on *a field of competitive play* between two teams. Third, I introduced the idea of *heroes and villains* in farm policy, battling for our progressive and conservative values. Finally, I empowered you with the idea of *the consumer-voter* who controls industry *and* government. It seems fitting to return to these four concepts as we consider what that might mean for food policy, partisan politics, foodies and farmers.

Food Policy is Technical

Voting with your fork requires technical knowledge to do it well. Voters want their choice to match their true preference, and this is not always easy in public policy settings. Sadly, many fans simply support the team, instead of supporting the policy goals, since it takes so much more effort to learn about policy goals.

Fans will simply support the red or blue team, perhaps based on some vague messaging from the players. Fans often do not think harder or take the time to learn about how policy really works on the ground. Providing for the social welfare is an economic undertaking. Economics is the study of the allocation of scarce resources, and it generally values the ability of a well-functioning market to allocate efficiently. However, markets can "fail" and this is where government "intervention" becomes attractive. When we look at where, when and how government can "intervene" in our food policy to allocate scarce resources in a manner consistent with our values, we see the long list of contemporary Farm Bill programs:

- *Commodity support* for grains, dairy, sugar, etc. with complicated formulas (historically based on parity, now "decoupled" from actual production in many cases)
- *Conservation* of land and water (with complicated government programs)
- *Trade* policy
- *Nutrition* assistance (again with complicated rules and formulas)
- *Credit*
- *Rural development* (usually in the form of grants for firms, organizations, and local governments)
- *Research* (targeted to the needs of the time)
- *Forestry*
- *Energy* promotion
- *Horticulture* programs
- *Crop Insurance* (again with complicated risk management rules and formulas)
- and a host of *Miscellaneous* needs and wants.

Political parties have staked out positions on many of these technical programs, and the Republican Party has been the most explicit, lately, about its support (or opposition) for the details of these programs. Does this mean Republican fans are more technically interested in food policy? It might, if food policy means food *production* policy. Historically both teams took technical positions on these issues, and it is interesting that Democrats are significantly less detailed in their party platforms when it comes to food policy. It might be interesting to see if similar vagaries hold for other non-food issues, or if this is only food related.

Being vague or being specific can also be a sign of disagreement on an issue. Perhaps Republicans are much more united in their approach to food policy, making it easier for them to agree on the details in writing. Thus, we see *substantive* commitments in Republican Party platforms. Perhaps Democrats keep things general and *symbolic* to unite on principle but to avoid disagreement on details. This can make things easier or harder for the progressive voter. It is easier because supporting or opposing a symbolic statement takes little effort or knowledge. It is harder because it might not be clear what that will mean on the ground, in family and farm life. It might *sound* good, but is it *good*? How do we know for sure? When Democrats were just as technical, we knew just what goals they would pursue when elected. Do their fans want to give them a blank food check, with only general principles? If so, why not ask for technical details? This is why the teasers from 2014 were so interesting. We can exactly picture the SNAP budget for families at 5% less (Republican) or .05% less (Democrat). We can exactly see Conservation spending at 8% less (Republican) or 5% less (Democrat).

Farm Policy is about Fielding a Team

Voting really matters to our players on the field. In fact, we learned that partisan *farm* policy is really *field* policy—what will keep the team *on the field*. And, interestingly enough, this has a lot to do with what is in the fields and on the tables (and on the menus, and in the refrigerator, and for sale at the store or local farmers market) where the players are elected. In other words, political teams want to be re-elected so they can keep making political plays.

National Teams, National Issues

As we learned, the national team takes a national view. These are the players like Presidents and Speakers and Senate Majority Leaders that have national followings and national constituencies. Because they are national leaders, they want to sell their party to the voters. This means having consistent principles, such as an ideology (conservative or liberal) and an agenda. This party agenda is most easily seen in the party platforms, what we called the team play book. The party platform lists the key ideas and agenda items that should define the teams approach on the field.

Democratic leaders have a national agenda formulated around economic security, equality, environmental protection. Each of these items informs their approach to food and farm policy. As a supporter of economic security and social welfare policies (including farm policy) since the New Deal, the Democratic party wants to use government to support family farmers (especially small farmers) and to support families more generally with SNAP funding and other low-income food programs for the elderly, foodbanks, schools and farmer's markets. As for equality, the recent Democratic Party has pushed for programs to benefit "historically disadvantaged farmers" such as minorities and women and young farmers. As for the environment, the national agenda calls for supporting farm practices and food policy that provides cleaner water and clean air, that protects national lands, that "combats" climate change. The ideology in this is a community-minded government approach.

Republican leaders have a national agenda formulated around economic prosperity, freedom, and practical use of natural resources. Like Democrats, these items inform their approach to food and farm policy. As a supporter of economic prosperity, they support free-market approaches to food and fiber (timber, cotton, hemp, wool) production, including less subsidies, free trade, and less regulation of market transactions, contracts and prices. In the Republican mind, prosperous industry leads to prosperous people who have the most efficient, abundant, safe food system in the world. As for freedom, this freedom applies to the farmer-business operator, to the property owner, to the firms who operate in this market—literally "freedom" to farm & produce for a consuming population. As for natural resources, the national agenda calls for keeping those resources in the marketplace for practical use with practical pollution prevention—especially the ability to use land and water for food and fiber production.

What is interesting about these national agendas is, as alluded to in the beginning of this book, *both lists* are important if nations and citizens of those nations want to eat. Combining the list is the national food agenda: economic security and economic prosperity, equality and freedom, environmental protection and practical use of natural resources. As a popular bumper sticker in farm country says "No Farms, No Food." And those farms need *all of the above* to provide that food. That all of the above means that emphasizing one will necessarily limit the other, and this is how political competition has sorted the parties into separate teams, on opposite ends of the field, with opposite political goals. However, it seems obvious that what is in the fields and on the tables requires healthy helpings of both approaches to feed a nation.

In the past, much of this policy was directed at the *pitchfork* crowd—farm families and their rural communities: families and communities who needed economic security and prosperity, farm families who wanted equality and freedom, farm families who were asked to conserve the resources they used. Political parties traditionally responded to the pitchfork crowd since farmers and rural voters where important voting blocs in seasonal elections. Democrats courted the pitchforks with farm support programs. Republicans courted the pitchforks with farm freedom programs.

Now, many policies are directed at the *dinner fork* crowd—those who eat. Unlike the old days, those who farm and those who live in rural communities are a much smaller group. To win elections, parties must appeal to the majority of voters, and that has been done with more emphasis on the values of urban and suburban voters. These voters want better social welfare programs, less subsidies (more free market) for businesses like farming, more conservation efforts, more support for non-traditional food and fiber products (fruits/vegetables, aquaculture, hemp), innovative production methods (urban farming, organic, cage-free/free-range, grass-fed), and community distribution (local, direct-marketing support). Keeping a team on the field requires political parties to cater to dinner fork values.

Local Representatives, Local Needs

As we also learned, the member of Congress and the Senator takes a local view. This means the player on the field has her eye on her fans in the stands. For the House member, this means thinking hard about the voting district—a geographic place with a particular economy, people, values, and needs. For a Senator, this means thinking hard about the State—also a particular economy, people, values and needs. Even for a House member and a Senator from the same state, things can look different. My member of the House looks at the Shenandoah Valley, a modestly prosperous countryside with a diverse farming & small manufacturing base. My member of the Senate sees a state that stretches from a heavily populated, prosperous Northern Virginia to Chesapeake Bay-dependent military-dominated industries in Norfolk-Hampton Roads, to a thinly populated piedmont and mountain region with many suffering and boarded-up little towns. Think about your own state, and you can see the same difference in scope for your member of Congress and your Senator. Just from this experiment, you can see why House members might be more parochial than Senators.

These parochial views are also a lot more practical or *material* in nature. Ideology just can't compete with realities on the ground. Thus a Democratic Senator and a Republican House member will be at the same ribbon-cutting for a large factory, both discussing jobs and community prosperity. Both will work on local economic and social problems, both will address constituent and firm needs, and both will speak sensitively about local values. In the case of food policy, farm groups and community food groups forge relationships with local representatives, no matter their jersey—both need their support—and Democrats and Republicans take pride in serving local people and firms, often telling colleagues "But what about the people in my district or state?"

Like the national team, these players want to stay on the field, so it is partly for reelection support. However, It is about more than that. Dedicated members of the House (or Senate) also wants to serve and make a difference for their territory—they want it to prosper. This can unite players around values, needs, problems, perspectives foreign to national leaders but very real to the players on the ground—often vexing party strategy and leading to historically rogue bi-partisan blocks in Congress. This is how we have seen much more moderate, practical policy arise in the farm bill. No extreme ideological agenda has taken hold since *all of the above* is necessary for ground operation. Now, if the people become more ideological than practical, this could pose a threat to the system. Those fans would continually seek to replace practical players with ideological ones, perhaps making practical players *turn* ideological—and in my view—

threatening the material, practical system on which food production and distribution depends. Ideas and aspirations improve our approaches, but they cannot feed us.

In modern times, things are still pretty practical. The dinner fork crowd and the pitchfork crowd have practical, material issues policy is capable of balancing. A healthy dose of consumer-producer relations in the market economy helps with some of this. Cage-free eggs and non-GMO foods were provided by the market first, due to consumer demand. A healthy dose of government regulation, especially of market externalities like conservation and environmental protection, consumer protection, food safety, and anti-competitive monopolies also helps keep the free-market functioning as it should. Programs such as SNAP, school lunch, and farm market support also use private firms and market forces to enhance nutrition programming. Programs such as conservation reserve programs (CREP), farmland easement programs, and cost-share EQIP farm-level environmental protection programs likewise use market forces to enhance environmental protection. These programs serve local needs for local representatives, but also preserve many national agenda items. We can see economic security and prosperity, we can see equality and freedom, we can see environmental protection and practical resource use.

Moving toward the Middle of the Field

As we have seen, political parties consistently move toward the middle of the field on many food issues. In our 2014 teaser, both parties supported more crop insurance, less SNAP spending, less conservation spending, much less commodity spending. These reflected the national values during the Great Recession, a need to reduce government spending. In our discussion of Congress and presidents, both teams consistently argued and voted to help the farm economy, help the environment and help needy families. In fact, half of the farm bills were also bi-partisan—gaining a majority of support from both parties. Moreover, the level of agreement in party platforms likewise demonstrated Democrat and Republican support for "age-old farm needs" in technical farm support programs, support for USDA conservation programs, and support for nutrition and health. A side-by-side comparison of party platforms demonstrated much more agreement than disagreement. These findings are consistent with classic political science notions of the "median voter." If most fans are moderate and "in the middle", that is where the team will move. Extreme teams risk attracting only extreme fans, and losing elections, so they move to the middle to attract more votes and to keep their team on the field.

Fan Voting

Unlike the technical discussion above, this leads us to a different conclusion. Namely, no matter which way I vote, food policy likely will not move that much.

It will stay near the fifty-yard line (in the middle). This is true in the short-term. However, long-term analysis of food policy has demonstrated quite a shift in policy. A Democrat or Republican from the 1930's would hardly recognize farm policy in 2020. The principles are there, but the details have moved drastically. Support payments are way down (100% parity anyone?). Nutrition assistance is way up (80% of the farm bill?). Conservation compliance has moved from regulatory (New Deal) to voluntary (1990s) to mandatory for all USDA farms (2018). This shift in policy has kept pace with the population—five times the number of Americans receive nutrition assistance (~12%) than farm for a living (2%). The shift has also kept pace with a new appreciation for the environment as a resource to be protected. Where historic property owners once may have felt they can do anything they want with their property, today's owners understand they have an environmental responsibility and they *want* to be good stewards of the land. They just want reasonable, technically feasible environmental solutions—and the Republican Party has been more sensitive to the technical needs of producers, making it the farmer's party.

For this reason, farmers vote the details, while the rest of the fans simply vote the jersey (out of habit) knowing general food policy won't change that much. And, if it does, the fans can always rein in a rogue team by threatening to take their votes elsewhere. However, the parties do have distinct approaches to food policy, and Republican or Democratic control for a while does move policy *incrementally* toward more redder or bluer goals. This means foodies and farmers should pay attention to the details when they vote. *Those details and that fine print matter on the ground and in the kitchen.* Ignoring technical ideas means ignoring the ideas—with little sense of where a party might actually take food policy. In this spirit, Democratic fans would do well to demand more of their team on this issue. This also means food policy does swing right to left every few years or so, but not too far on most issues most years. However, over the long haul, the swings are much more noticeable, so small victories can lead to significant gains in policy direction. Public policy scholars have long documented that policies, once enacted, have their own inertia, tend to grow in size and scope, and rarely are terminated. These seemingly small changes often add up to big movement after a few administrations and Congresses go by. In this way, voting with your fork means being deliberate and choosy, not just ordering the Blue Plate Special or the Red Daily Deal and hoping for something good.

Farm Policy Creates Heroes and Villains

Most folks who run for President, Senate or House do not think much about their food policy legacy, but they should. Here is a place where a candidate can literally make a difference on those "kitchen table" issues so many Americans worry about, with bonuses for healthcare and the environment—legacies often much more at the top of a candidate's profile. Food policy also offers a legacy for fiscal responsibility, the economy and jobs—all of the issues the typical candidate might embrace. Food provision is a public service, even when it is done with private property and capital. Farmers, grocers, food processors, restaurants and non-profits are rightfully proud of their role in feeding people. In the pandemic crisis of 2020, these citizens and firms were second only to healthcare workers and hospitals for national prominence and government intervention. Government wanted to keep food available, using national and local policy in a "how can we help?" approach. Candidates and officials should keep this mindset when approaching their food policy legacy. Fans should encourage their candidates to develop a food legacy by asking questions and demanding approaches. In 2020, Bernie Sanders was the most explicit and technically savvy food legacy candidate. However, President Donald Trump ended up with the most important food policy moves in a lifetime (trade, environment, pandemic policy, etc.). Likely neither candidate's supporters (except farmers) thought much about these candidates' potential food legacy.

USDA Secretaries also figure prominently in our nation's food policy legacy. Most fans never even consider a candidate's cabinet choices, let alone the secretary of Agriculture—almost always a politician from a farm state with a farm background. However, USDA secretaries do think about their food policy legacy. Potential cabinet members from farm states should dream big and reach out to Presidential candidates with their ideas for a food legacy. Voters from farm states have an outsized role in food policy simply because they likely vetted USDA secretaries when the food legacy leaders were *mere* Governors or Senators or other elected officials. Sometimes these secretaries were state-level agricultural officials, serving on a sort of JV team with limited jurisdiction and more parochial food policy experience. One can imagine that a Secretary from Vermont would look very different than a Secretary from Kansas or California. Voting with your fork means thinking hard about what chef you want in the White House kitchen cabinet: who should that person be? What skills and values should they have? What experience would best serve the nation?

The Power of the Consumer-Voter

As we saw in the past, food issues were front and center for voters. Today, it is the consumer who is making changes and wielding the most power. Many changes in food production are arising in the private sector, driven by consumer preferences and corporate response. And this makes a lot of sense. If the free market provides the food, the citizen's role in the free market as a consumer is where quite a bit of power might lie.

The preceding chapters have demonstrated the power of ordinary people in partisan politics. Those who pay attention and care about food issues, like foodies and farmers, can easily obtain the attention of government officials *because of* competitive party play. Political party leaders and local representatives in the House and the Senate are keenly interested in what "folks back home" think. The team needs your support to stay in office, and they are willing to work for it.

The preceding chapters also demonstrated the awesome power of the people to check "rogue" players and teams, swinging elections and fortunes on a key food policy issue. In recent times, rural issues have kept the attention of the Republican Party because much of their voting base is rural—for President, the House and the Senate. Even anti-farm Republican Presidents (including Bush and Trump) have been generous with farm benefits to keep support in rural America. By contrast, the Democratic Party has felt much less pressure on food issues, and their efforts show it. They have a loyal farm block in Congress, but those seem to be the only Democrats concerned about food, except for, perhaps, supporting First Lady Michelle Obama's and Hunger-Healthy Free Kids in 2010 or defending SNAP in 2014 and 2018. None of those policies likely garnered a sense of new support for the Party however. Why do food issues seem so marginal among Democratic voters? I believe the answer lies in the basic complacency of abundance. We can take food for granted in this country, and I suspect even needy voters would not cite food support as a reason to cast their vote for Democrats. The connection between party and food is just not there for the ordinary voter. I also believe the answer is because both parties do quite a bit for our food policy, so this, too, keeps the electoral stakes lower. Neither party runs on a *food* platform. The Republicans run on an *agriculture* platform, which sounds distant and remote to most voters. In this spirit, I believe there is quite a bit of room of party entrepreneurs to be more explicit and tap into the food interests of voters. It is my hope that this book will help even *candidates* learn the history of their party and food issues, so that they can better represent us by mastering this fundamental political issue. Political leaders from ancient times have always possessed a healthy appreciation for their food legacy. American political leaders and citizen voters should do the same.

Addendum: Some Notes for My Social Science Friends

For those academics who are interested in food issues (agriculture economists, public health researchers, anthropologists, sociologists and so on), I wanted to provide a little perspective from political science theory since experts in one discipline are often unfamiliar with literatures in other disciplines. You many find these theoretical approaches useful. This book is a descriptive and analytical work of political parties and food & farm policy. When a scholar is looking into a question, she might draw from several theories to know where to look and what to look for. In the question of partisanship and food policy, I looked to four theoretical literatures and understandings in the field of political science.

Defining Partisanship

For starters, the book takes *political science definitions of partisanship* from Congressional scholars Hurwitz, Moiler & Rhode (2001) who define a partisan issue as one where the majorities of each party vote in opposite directions on a bill--Parties moving in opposite directions or advocating opposite approaches.

Thinking about Political Parties

One key theoretical approach is based on a political science understanding of parties behaving in an institutional electoral context—a geographic nation electing leadership to the national legislature and the national executive. Party Scholars since Morris Fiorina have examined party in three parts: the voters, the party organization, and the party in government. In creating my own theory of politics as a sport, I rename these categories the fans (voters) the coaches (RNC DNC) and the players (House, Senators, Presidents, etc.) I also discuss the "sponsors" of the game (lobbyists) and "Cinderella teams" (third parties, like the Populist Party of the 1890's). In this context of electoral competition (sport), legislative & executive leaders have different goals than the rank-in-file members of Congress who hail from local districts with local needs. This difference between the ideological *principles* of agenda driven leadership (House Speaker, President—who need agendas to win as a national party) and the *parochial practical needs* of rank-in-file members (Representatives & Senators—who need to meet local needs) explains much of the way political parties have crafted and supported food policy. This conception of the Sport of electoral competition is explained in Ch. 2 and used in each of the other chapters.

Thinking about Social Welfare Policy

A second theoretical approach is my own extension of interest group scholar Adam Sheingate's *The Rise of the Agricultural Welfare State* (2001) and presidential scholars Smith and Seltzer *Polarization and the Presidency: From FDR to Obama* (2015) on political parties. Sheingate's analysis of the history of farm policy development documents the reality of farm policy as a social welfare policy. Smith and Seltzer do not analyze farm policy but offer the theory that parties have divided themselves on social welfare policy (and race policy). I marry the two to say if social welfare policy is a partisan fault line (Smith and Seltzer) and farm policy is social welfare policy (Sheingate) then farm policy must be partisan when it acts as a social welfare policy (Harris—me!).

Thinking about Morality Policy

A third theoretical approach is my own "hunch" that food policy has several unique dimensions in partisan politics. Discussed in Ch. 6, these dimensions draw on "morality policy" Scholarship of Chris Mooney (2000), the "issue evolution" scholarship of Carmines and Stimson's (1989) classic work and the newer "issue ownership" scholarship. These approaches treat "morality" policy as separate from economic or practical policy, and they see parties as having legitimate "ownership" over certain issues in the eyes of the voting public (e.g., Democrats own Environmental policy or Republicans own National Security policy). So what about Food policy? If is it is moral, it might separate parties differently than if it is economic. Does either party have "issue ownership" over food issues?

Thinking about Political Party Platforms

A fourth theoretical literature is the political science approach to party platforms and how to analyze them. John Aldrich (2011) resurrected the idea that parties matter. A separate literature (e.g., Oliver and Marion, 2008) on party platforms sees platforms as having symbolic and substantive statements playing different roles in the platform, and a classic party literature expects parties to converge in their policy approach (Anthony Downs 1954). Combining these approaches, I look to see where parties converge/diverge symbolically and substantively.

References

2012 Election Map (County Level) http://politicalmaps.org/2012-electoral-map/

Abler, David. 1989. "Vote Trading on Farm Legislation in the U.S. House." *American Journal of Agricultural Economics.* 71:583-591.

Ball, Molly. 2014. "How Republicans Lost the Farm." *The Atlantic.* January 27, 2014.

Barker, Allen V. 2010. Science and Technology of Organic Farming. New York: CRC Press.

Barnes, Bart. 1988. Barry Goldwater, GOP Hero, Dies. *The Washington Post* May 30, 1998. https://www.washingtonpost.com/archive/politics/1998/05/30/barry-goldwater-gop-hero-dies/22107068-2842-4505-bb1d-ec9e4783d206/?utm_term=.5b6bae796c92 Last accessed May 31, 2017.

Bittman, Mark et al. 2014. How a National Food Policy could save millions of lives. The Washington Post. November 7, 2014.

Botterill, Linda Courtnenay. 2004. "Valuing Agriculture: Balancing Competing Objectives in the Policy Process." *Journal of Public Policy* 24(2):199-218.

Browne William and K. Paik. 1993. Beyond the Domain: Recasting Network Politics in the Post Reform Congress. American Journal of Political Science 37: pp. 1054-1078.

Bump, Philip. 2014. "There really are Two Americas. An Urban one and a Rural one." *The Washington Post* October 21, 2014.

Carmines, Edward G. and James A. Stimson. 1980. "The Two Faces of Issue Voting." *American Political Science Review.* 74:78-91.

Carmines, Edward G. and James A. Stimson. 1989. *Issue Evolution: Race and the Transformation of American Politics.* Princeton, NJ: Princeton University Press

Centner, Terence C. 2004. Empty Patures: Confined Animals and the Transformation of the Rural Landscape. Urbana, IL: University of Illinois Press

Clinton, William J. 1996. Statement on Signing the Federal Agricultural Improvement and Reform Act of 1996. April 4, 1996. Online by Gerhard Peters and John T. Woolley, The American Presidency Project. http://www.presidency.ucsb.edu/ws?pid=52628 accessed December 8, 2016.

Confessore, Nicholas. 2014. "How School Lunch Became the Latest Political Battleground." *The New York Times.* October 7, 2014.

Clift, Eleanor. 1985. Reagan Sign's History's Most Costly Farm Bill. LA Times. December 24, 1985. http://articles.latimes.com/1985-12-24/news/mn-20869_1_farm-bill
(Last Accessed November 30, 2016.)

Constance, Douglas Harbin et al. 2013. "Social Dimensions of Organic Production and System Research." Crop Management. 12 (1): Dec 2013.

Converse, Phillip E. 1964. "The Nature of Belief Systems in Mass Publics." In *Ideology and Discontent*, edited by David E. Apter. New York: Free Press.

Cox, Gary, and Matthew McCubbins. 1993. *Legislative Leviathan.* University of California Press.

Cox, Gary, and Matthew McCubbins. 2005. *Setting the Agenda.* New York: Cambridge University Press

Bawn, Kathleen et al. 2012. "A Theory of Political Parties: Groups, Policy Demands and Nominations in American Politics," Perspectives on Politics, 10(3):571-597 at 575.

Derthick, Martha. 1970 *The Influence of Federal Grants: Public Assistance in Massachusetts* (Cambridge MA: Harvard University Press).

Dunlap, Riley E. and Micheal Patrick Allen. 1976. "Partisan Differences on Environmental Issues: A Congressional Roll-Call Analysis." *Western Political Quarterly* 29:384-397.

De Lama, George and Lea Donosky. 1985. "Regan Kills Farm Bill: No bailout for farmers in debt." Chicago Tribune March 7, 1985.
http://articles.chicagotribune.com/1985-03-07/news/8501130185_1_veto-farm-programs-farmers (Last accessed November 30, 2016).

Eberstadt, Mary. 2009. Is Food the New Sex? Policy Review (Hoover Institution) February & March 2009.

Eidenmuller, Michael E. 2008. Transcript of Ronald Reagan, A Time for Choosing delivered October 27th 1964.
http://www.americanrhetoric.com/speeches/ronaldreaganatimeforchoosing.htm Last accessed October 20, 2016.

Finchbaugh, Barry and Ron Knutson. 2004. "The Agriculture Policy Outlook: Looking Back Focuses the Road Ahead." *Choices.* 2004 (4) pp. 27-29.

Fiorina, Morris P. 1980. "The Decline of Collective Responsibility in American Politics," *Daedalus* 71: 883-917.

Fiorina, Morris P. 2004. "What Culture Wars?" *Wall Street Journal.* July 14, 2004.

Flammang, Janet A. 2009. A Taste for Civilization. Urbana: University of Illinois Press

Freeman, Patricia K. 1985. Interstate communication among state legislators regarding energy policy innovation. Publius. 15:99-111.

Freshwater, David and Jordan Leising. 2015. "Why Farm Support Persists: An Explanation Grounded in Congressional Political Economy." Paper presented at the Southern Agricultural Economics Association's 2015 meeting.

Gallup. 2011. "Americans Oppose Cuts in Education, Social Security and Defense." Gallup Poll Report January 26, 2011. http://www.gallup.com/poll/145790

Gardener, Bruce L. 2002. American Agriculture in the Twentieth Century. Cambridge: Harvard University Press.

Gilbert, J. and Oladi R. 2012. "Net Campaign Contributions, Agricultural Interests, and Votes on Liberalizing Trade with China." *Public Choice* 150:745-769.

Glick, Henry and Scott P. Hayes. 1991. Innovation and reinvention in state policymaking: Theory and the evolution of living wills. *The Journal of Politics* 53:835-50.

Glassman, Marcus. 2015. Hungry for Information: Polling Americans on Their Trust in the Food System. Chicago Council on Global Affairs. October 2015. https://www.thechicagocouncil.org/publication/hungry-information-polling-americans-their-trust-food-system Last accessed May 2, 2017.

Goble, Hannah and Peter M. Holm. 2009. "Breaking Bonds? The Iraq War and the Loss of Republican Dominance in National Security." Political Research Quarterly 62:215-229.

Gonzalez, Sarah. 2012. "Agri-Pulse Poll shows most farmers will vote Romney, blame Democrats on Farm Bill." *Agri-Pulse* 11-5-12.

Gray, Virginia. 1973. Innovation in the states: A diffusion study. The American Political Science Review 67:1174-85.

Gruber, Philip. 2015. "Hen Cages Fare Well in Layer Study." *Lancaster Farming.* April 18, 2015 p. A5.

Guebert, Alan. 2004. "Reagan Planted today's ag seeds." Farm and Dairy. June 16, 2004. http://www.farmanddairy.com/columns/reagan-planted-todays-ag-seeds/6301.html
(Last Accessed November 30, 2016).

Hagstrom, Jerry. 2017. "Senators: No Farm Bill Cuts." The Progressive Farmer. May 26, 2017.

Hanavan, Louise, Chloe Kennedy and Greg Cameron. 2010. "And now for the Main Course: A Critique of the Popular Food and Farm Literature." Humboldt Journal of Social Relations.33: 166-188.

Hand, Michael S. and Stephen Martinez. 2010. "Just What does Local Mean?" Choices 25 (1) http://www.choicesmagazine.org

Hansen, John Mark. 1991. *Gaining Access: Congress and the Farm Lobby.* Chicago: University of Chicago Press.

Harmon, Amy. 2014. Lonely Quest for Facts on Genetically Modified Foods. New York Times January 4. 2014. Noting 20 states had bills pending. See also Strong Support for Labeling Modified Foods. New York Times. July 27, 2013.

Harris, Rebecca C. 2015. "State responses to biotechnology: Legislative action and policymaking in the U.S., 1990-2010." *Politics and the Life Sciences* 34: 1-29.

Harris, Rebecca C. 2016. The Political Identity of Food: Partisan Implications of the New Food Politics." Food Studies: An Interdisciplinary Journal 6(4):1-20.

Haskell, John. 2010. *Congress in Context.* Boulder CO: Westview Press.

Haspel, Tamara. 2014. "Farm Bill: Why don't taxpayers subsidize the foods that are better for us? *The Washington Post* February 18, 2004.

Heclo, Hugh. 1978. "Issue Networks and the Executive Establishment." in The New American Political System ed. Anthony King, 870124. Washington, D. C.: American Enterprise Institute

Hershey, Marjorie, and Paul Allen Beck. 2004. *Party Politics in America* (11th) White Plains, NY: Longman Publishing Group.

Hofferbert, Richard I. and John K. Urice. 1985. "Small-Scale policy: Federal Stimulus versus Competing Explanations for State Funding of the Arts." *American Journal of Political Science* 29:308-29.

Hopkinson, Jenny. 2014. "Monsanto Confronts Devilish Public Image Problem." *Politico* November 29, 2013 http://dyn.politico.com

Hudson, William E. 2012. *American Democracy in Peril: Eight Challenges to America's Future.* Los Angeles: CQ Press

Hurwitz, Mark S., Roger J. Moiles and David W. Rohde. 2001. Distributive and Partisan Issues in Agricultural Policy in the 104th House," *American Political Science Review* 95:911-922.

Imhoff, Daniel. 2012. *Food Fight: The Citizen's Guide to the Next Food and Farm Bill* (2nd). Healdsburg, CA: Watershed Media.

James, Randy. 2013. Why Cows Need Names: and more secrets of Amish farming. Kent, OH: Kent State Univeristy Press

Jasanoff, Shelia. 2006. "Biotechnology and Empire: The Global Power of Seeds and Science." Osiris, 2nd 21:273-292.

Jefferson, Thomas. 1964. *Notes On the State of Virginia* New York, NY: Harper and Row Publishers.

Judis, John B. "Tea Minus Zero," *The New Republic*, May 27, 2010.

Kamieniecki, Sheldon. 1995. "Political Parties and Environmental Policy" in *Environmental Politics and Policy: Theories and Evidence*, James P. Lester (ed.) Durham, NC: Duke University Press.

Key, V.O. 1967. *Parties, Pressure Groups and Politics*. New York: Crowell Company.

Kleiman, Jordan. 2009. "Local Food and the Problem of Public Authority." Technology and Culture. 50:399-417.

Kleiman, Jordan. 2009. "Local Food and the Problem of Public Authority." *Technology and Culture*. 50:399-417.

Knutson, Ronald D. 2007. Agricultural and Food Policy (6th). Upper Saddle River NJ: Pearson Prentice Hall.

Knutson, Ronald D., David Schweikhardt, and Edward Smith. 2002. Political Setting for the 2002 Farm Bill.
http://www.iatp.org/files/Political_Setting_for_the_2002_Farm_Bill.htm
Last accessed January 6, 2017.

Kopicki, Allison. 2013. "Strong Support for Labeling Modified Foods." *New York Times*. July 27, 2013.

Krutz, Glen S. 2005. "Issues and Institutions: 'Winnowing' in the U.S. Congress." *American Journal of Political Science* 49:313-326.

Lang, Tim and Michael Heasman. 2004. *Food Wars: The Global Battle for Mouths, Minds, and Markets*. London: Earthscan

Laws, Forrest. 2017. "Health care battle may presage next farm bill debate" Southest Farm Press. May 3, 2017. P. 4.

Lee, Frances E. 2008. "Dividers, Not Uniters: Presidential Leadership and Senate Partisanship, 1981-2004." *Journal of Politics* 70:914-928.

Lowi, Theodore J. 1964. "American Business, Public Policy, Case Studies and Political Theory." *World Politics* 16:667-715.

Lowi, Theodore J. 1964. "How the farmers get what they want," *Reporter* May 21, 1964 pp. 34-37.

Lowi, Theodore. 1972. "Four systems of Policy, Politics, and Choice." Public Administration Review 32:298-310.

Lusk, Jayson. 2013. *The Food Police: A Well-fed Manifesto About the Politics of Your Plate*. New York: Crown Forum.

Lyson, Thomas A. 2004. *Civic Agriculture: Reconnecting Farm, Food and Community*. Medford, MA: Tufts University Press.

McConnell, Grant. 1966. *Private Power and American Democracy*. New York: Alfred A. Knopf chapter 7.

McCune, Wesley. 1943. *The Farm Bloc.* Garden City, NY: Doubleday, Doran and
    Company, Inc
Meier, Kenneth J. 2001. *The Public Clash of Private Values: The Politics of Morality
    Policy.* Chatham, NJ: Chatham House.
Mercier, S.S. 2011. "External Factors that will drive the next Farm Bill debate." *Choices.*
Miller, Edward Alan. 2004. "Advancing Comparative State Policy Research: Toward
    Conceptual Integration and Methodological Expansion." *State and Local
    Government Review* 36:35-58.
Mintrom, Michael. 2008. Competitive Federalism and the Governance of Controversial
    Science. The Journal of Federalism. 39:606-631.
Mooney, Chris Z. 2000. "The Decline of Federalism and the Rise of Morality-Policy
    Conflict in the United States. *Publius.* 30:171-188.
Mooney, Christopher Z. 2000. "The Decline of Federalism and the Rise of Morality-
    Policy Conflict in the United States." Publius. 30:171-188
Mooney, Christopher Z. and Richard G. Schuldt. 2008. "Does Morality Policy Exist?"
    Policy Studies Journal 36:199-216.
Murphy, Kevin. 2014. An Illiberal Education: 10 Critical lessons about the state of the
    food-system education in American Colleges and Universities.
    http://www.truthinfood.com
National Farmers Union. 2016. The Farmer's Share. https://nfu.org/farmers-share/ Last
    Accessed May 2, 2017.
National Research Council. 1989. Alternative Agriculture. Washington, DC: National
    Academy Press.
Nestle, Marion. 2013. *Food Politics: How the Food Industry Influences Nutrition and
    Health* (3rd) Berkeley, CA: University of California Press
Neustadt, Richard. 1960. *Presidential Power.* New York: John Wiley & Sons, Inc.
New York Times. "Senate Passes Farm Bill with Clear Winners and Losers." *New York
    Times.* February 4, 2014.
Norwood, F. Bailey, and Jayson Lusk. 2011. *Compassion by the Pound: The Economics of
    Farm Animal Welfare.* Oxford: Oxford University Press
Novak, James, James W. Pease and Larry D. Sanders. 2015. Agricultural Policy in the
    United States: Evolution and Economics. New York: Routledge.
Odum, Lance L. 2012. "Partisan Politics, Agricultural Interests and Effects on State-level
    Ethanol Subsidies." Open SIUC Research Papers. Paper 324.
    http://opensiuc.lib.siu.edu/gs_rp/324
Odum, Lance. L. 2012. "Partisan Politics, Agricultural Interests and Effects on State-level
    Ethanol Subsidies." Research Papers. Paper 324
    <http://opensiuc.lib.siu.edu/gs_rp/324
Outlaw, Joe L., James W. Richardson, Steven L. Klose. 2011. "Farm Bill Stakeholders:
    Competitors or Collaborators?" Choices 26 (2) http://www.choicesmagazine.org
Pennock, J. Roland. 1956. "Party and constituency in postwar agricultural price support
    legislation." Journal of Politics 18:171-181 (May 1956)
Petrocik, J.R. 1996. "Issue Ownership in Presidential Elections, with a 1980 Case Study."
    American Journal of Political Science 40:825-850.
Petrocik, John R., William L. Benoit, Glenn J. Hansen. 2003. "Issue Ownership and
    Presidential Campaigning, 1952-2000." *Political Science Quarterly* 188:599-626.
Pew Research Center. 2015. "A Deep Dive into Party Affiliation" April 7, 2015
    http://www.people-press.org/2015/04/07/a-deep-dive-into-party-affiliation/ last
    accessed March 17, 2017.

Plein, L. Christopher. 1991. "Popularizing Biotechnology: The Influence of Issue Definition." *Science, Technology & Human Values* 16:474-490.

Plumer, Brad. 2013. "The U.S. has few farmers. So why does Congress love farm subsidies?" *Washington Post.* July 12, 2013.

Pollan, Michael. 2006. The Ominvore's Dilemma: A Natural History of Four Meals. New York, NY: The Penguin Press.

Pollan, Michael. 2010. Food Movement, Rising. New York Review of Books, May 20. 2010.

Pringle, Peter. 2003. *Food, Inc.: Mendel to Monsanto—The Promises and Perils of the Biotech Harvest.* New York: Simon and Schuster.

Rae, Nicol. 2007. "Be Careful what you wish for: The Rise of Responsible Parties in American National Politics." Annual Review of Political Science. vol. 10.

Ranney, A. 1965. "Parties in State Politics," in *Politics in the American States.* H. Jacob & K. Vines (Eds.) Boston: Little, Brown.

Reagan, Ronald. 1985. Statement on Signing the Food Security Act of 1985. Public Papers of Ronald Reagan March 1985. Ronald Reagan Library. https://www.reaganlibrary.archives.gov/archives/speeches/1985/122385c.htm (Last accessed November 30, 2016).

Riedl, Brian M. 2002. "Agriculture Lobby Wins Big in New Farm Bill." Heritage Foundation Research Reports. April 9, 2002. http://www.heritage.org/research/reports/2002/04/agriculture-lobby-wins-big-in-new-farm-bill (Last Accessed January 6, 2017).

Salatin, Joel. 2007. *Everything I want to do is Illegal: War Stories from the Local Food Front.* Chelsea Green Publishing.

Schafer, Sam. 2012. "Nearly 200 Farmers share voting intentions." *Farm Journal* 10-18-12.

Schattschneider, E. E. 1960. *The Semi-Sovereign People.* New York: Holt, Rinehart and Winston

Schlesinger, Joseph A. 1975. "The Primary Goals of Political Parties: A Clarification of Positive Theory." *American Political Science Review* 69: 840-9.

Schlosser, Eric. 2001. *Fast Food Nation.* Boston: Houghton Mifflin Company.

Schneider, Anne L. et al. 2014. "Democratic Policy Design: Social Construction of Target Populations," in *Theories of the Policy Process*, Paul A. Sabatier and Christopher M. Wieble, editors. Westview Press.

Seabrook, Andrea. 2010. "CQ: 2009 Was The Most Partisan Year Ever." NPR January 11, 2010. http://www.npr.org.

Sheingate, Adam D. 2001. *The Rise of the Agriculture Welfare State.* Princeton University Press.

Sheingate, Adam D. 2006a. "Promotion Versus Precaution: The Evolution of Biotechnology Policy in the United States. British Journal of Political Science 36:243-268.

Sheingate, Adam D. 2006b. "Structure and Opportunity: Committee Jurisdiction and Issue Attention in Congress." American Journal of Political Science 50:844-859.

Skogstad, Grace. 2008. *Internationalization and Canadian Agriculture: Policy and Governing Paradigms.* Toronto: University of Toronto Press.

Smith, Mike. 2014. Ten Reasons Why They Hate You <http://www.truthinfood.com>

Smith, Robert C. and Richard A. Seltzer. 2015. Polarization and the Presidency: From FDR to Barak Obama. Boulder, CO: Lynne Rienner Publishers.

Smith, Vincent H. and Robert W. Goodman. 2015. "Should Washington End Agricultural Subsidies?" *The Wall Street Journal* July 15, 2015.

Souva, Mark, and David Rohde. 2007. "Elite Opinion Differences and Partisanship in Congressional Foreign Policy, 1975-1996," Political Research Quarterly 60:113-123.

Stabile, Bonnie. 2009. "What's the Matter with Kansas?" Politics and the Life Sciences 28:17-30.

Stephan, Hannes R. 2014. *Cultural Politics and the Transatlantic Divide over GMO's.* New York: Palgrave Macmillan.

Strom, Stephanie. 2014. They are Going to Wish They Could All be California Hens. (New York Times. March 4, 2014.) A1.

Summers, Mary. 1996. "Putting Populism Back In: Rethinking Agricultural Politics and Policy," *Agricultural History* Vol 70 No. 2 (Spring 1996) pp. 395-414.

Truman, David 1951. The Governmental Process New York: Knof

Tweeten, Luther. 2003. *Terrorism, Radicalism, and Populism in Agriculture.* Ames, IA: Iowa State Press.

Tweeten, Luther. 2003. *Terrorism, Radicalism, and Populism in Agriculture.* Ames, IA: Iowa State Press.

USDA. 2014. 2012 Census Highlights. May 2014
https://www.agcensus.usda.gov/Publications/2012/Online_Resources/Highlights/ Farm_Demographics/
Last Accessed May 2, 2017.

USDA. 2017. Ag Secretary Perdue Moves to Make School Meals Great Again. USDA Press release May 1, 2017.

Vogel, David. 1989. *Fluctuating Fortunes: The Political Power of Business in America.* New York: Basic Books.

Walker, Jack. 1969. "The Diffusion of Innovation among the American States." *American Political Science Review* 63:880-99.

Walker, Melissa. 2012. "Contemporary Agrarianism: A Reality Check." *Agricultural History* Vol. 86, No. 1 (Winter 2012) pp. 1-25.

Webber, David J. 1995. "The Emerging Federalism of U.S. Biotechnology Policy." *Politics and the Life Sciences* 14:65-72.

Weingast, Barry. 1979. "A Rational Choice Perspective on Congressional Norms." *American Journal of Political Science* 23:245-262.

Welch, Susan and Kay Thompson. 1980. The impact of Federal incentives on State Policy Innovation. *American Journal of Political Science*. 24:715-729.

Wilde, Parke E. 2014. "After Long Argument, Then Compromise, Congress Agrees on Nutrition Assistance Benefit Cuts in the Agricultural Act of 2014." *Choices* 29(2). http://www.choicesmagazine.org

Williams, Susan. 2006. Food in the United States, 1820-1890. Westport, Connecticut: Greenwood Press.

Wilson, James Q. 2006. "How Divided Are We? *Commentary* February 2006.

Wilson, James Q. 2006. "How Divided Are We?" *Commentary,* February 2006.

World Public Opinion. 2009. "Americans Oppose Most Farm Subsidies" *World Public Opinion.* April 22, 2009. http://www.worldpublicopinion.org

Aldrich, John A. Why parties? A Second Look, U of Chicago Press, 2011, p. 17

USDA Press Release July 24, 2018. "What they are Saying: Support for President Donald J. Trump's Plan to Protect American Farmers from Unjustified Trade Retaliation."

Duvall, Zippy. President of the American Farm Bureau Federation. Opposing View Op-Ed: Farmers need USDA Help, USA today, July 25, 2018.

"Ag Department to Send $12 Billion to Farmers hurt by Tariffs." Washington Post. July 24, 2018.

Oliver, Willlard M. and Nancy E. Marion. 2008. "Political Party Platforms: Symbolic Politics and Criminal Justice Policy," Criminal Justice Policy Review 19(4):397-413.

Downs, Anthony. 1957. An Economic Theory of Democracy. New York: Harper and Row.

CPSIA information can be obtained
at www.ICGtesting.com
Printed in the USA
LVHW070955050323
740957LV00011B/1328